MR. HOCKEY

MR. HOCKEY
The World of Gordie Howe

Don O'Reilly

Henry Regnery Company • Chicago

Copyright © 1975 by Don O'Reilly
All rights reserved
Published by Henry Regnery Company
180 North Michigan Avenue, Chicago, Illinois 60601
Manufactured in the United States of America
Library of Congress Catalog Card Number: 75-13237
International Standard Book Number: 0-8092-8273-9

Published simultaneously in Canada by
Fitzhenry & Whiteside Limited
150 Lesmill Road
Don Mills, Ontario M3B 2T5
Canada

To Howard, who "shoots" his hockey Southern style
And to Edith who tolerates this nonsense

Contents

1 Mr. Hockey 1
2 Born on the Farm 9
3 The Schoolboy Discovers Hockey 15
4 Painful Early Views of the Outside World 25
5 Debut at Olympia 35
6 On the Edge of Death 41
7 Love Bowls Him Over 45
8 Through His Admirers' Eyes 53
9 The Meanest? 59
10 Skills and Honors Escalate 67
11 "The Greatest of Them All!" 75
12 Success, Pain, and Humor 85
13 Red Wings Are Champions Again—
    for the Last Time! 93
14 Welcome Home and Other Rewards 101

15	A Couple of Milestones and Surgery	111
16	Another Two-Year Contract, and 100 Grand	123
17	Time for the Decision	129
18	The Two Greatest Honors for an Athlete	145
19	Out One Era and in Another	151
20	A Look Back—A Look Ahead	165
21	Career Number Two	175
22	"Playing for My Country!"	185
23	Another Milestone—A Big One!	189

With sincere gratitude to the Detroit Public Library for recognizing early the sports greatness of No. 9; to the dedicated and observing Detroit sportswriters who have been in the forefront of the Gordie Howe watchers from the beginning; to the magazine writers and radio and TV interviewers who have faithfully chronicled the Gordie Howe story for almost three decades; and to the amazing detailed recollections of the Howes of three generations as they talked with writers and broadcasters so many times.

To the Howes—Gordie, Colleen, Marty, Mark, Cathy, and Murray—a salute and a bow. To borrow and paraphrase a line from TV's Lou Gordon, "One of North America's finest families!"

D.E.O.

1

Mr. Hockey

"At first I worried about him because he seemed like a duck out of water."

That was the concern of 18-year-old Marty Howe as he watched his 45-year-old Dad, the greatest hockey player of all time, make an unprecedented comeback in professional competition after a voluntary two-year layoff.

Gordie Howe had come off the impoverished Canadian farmland, from the small town of Saskatoon in Western Canada, to sign with the Detroit Red Wings at age 16 (spending a couple of years in the Wings' farm system until he could reach the National Hockey League's legal age of 18).

During the next quarter century Gordie Howe became a sports legend wherever hockey was played. He became a national sports hero throughout Canada. In Detroit's sports history he ranked at the top, along with other legendary figures from the Motor City, such as baseball's great Ty

Cobb, boxing's heavyweight champion Joe Louis and auto racing's three-time Indy 500 winner Mauri Rose.

Someone wrote a song about him and the record was played on Detroit radio stations so often it seemed to be the city's own theme song—"Gordie Howe, the greatest of them all, yes the greatest of them all!"

In mid-summer 1971, Gordie Howe looked back on a great personal career in the N.H.L., but the joy of competition was gone. The front office of the Detroit hockey club had been split apart by friction and dissension and the once-great champion hockey team now had a losing record so bad the fans stayed away by the hundreds.

As long as the Red Wings were winners and there was teamwork and harmony among the players, Gordie Howe could overlook and live with the pain from the arthritis in both wrists. With the program rocketing downhill, the arthritis pain became almost unbearable, so Howe announced his retirement as an active player, after 25 years on the N.H.L. ice, and accepted a front-office job.

As might be expected, with all the Red Wings' management turmoil, the next two years were bittersweet for the always shy and introverted (off the ice) Howe. Conditions were generally unpleasant on the job as he was caught in the middle between old friends and new bosses, but enjoyable because at long last he could spend more time in the loving company of his wife and four children.

Moreover, the N.H.L. waived the three-year waiting rule and quickly inducted Gordie Howe into the National Hockey League Hall of Fame on the grounds of the Canadian National Exhibition in Toronto.

Now it was 1973, and Gordie Howe and the two older sons, Marty and Mark, had signed four-year contracts to play in the rival World Hockey League with the Houston Aeros.

Going into the first game of the season, Marty Howe was not the only person who was doubtful.

Said Mrs. Colleen Howe, the energetic family manager: "My thoughts as a wife were filled mainly with concern for Gordie's physical capabilities. I knew he would never settle for limited ice time, but after he passed a major medical examination, I felt better. I knew how important it was for Gordie to participate with his sons on a professional hockey team.

"An opportunity such as that would come to few, if any, in a lifetime, and he needed this experience to fulfill a dream that began so many years ago."

On the eve of the first game of the 1973-74 World Hockey Association season for the Houston Aeros, in that great Texas city, the middle-aged Gordie Howe was also doubtful. In fact, he was suffering real pain.

Less than 24 hours before the starting gun, Gordie Howe lay in traction in a Houston hospital, receiving treatment for a sprained back, a more or less normal problem for a 45-year-old veteran playing the brutal, vicious contact sport with youngsters, some of whom were young enough to be his sons.

"Oh, no! How can I go on like this?" Gordie asked himself again and again.

But the gutsy determination to accept the challenge had marked his more than 30-year sports career—in fact his entire life from childhood.

In 1950, just concluding his fourth year in the N.H.L., Gordie hovered on the edge of the precipice of death from injuries suffered in the playoffs leading to the Stanley Cup finals, but he came back the following season even stronger and more combative, on his way to superstar status and an honored niche in the National Hockey League Hall of Fame.

Although it hardly seems plausible to the casual observer, it appears that the contracts for the services of Gordie, Marty, and Mark, worth about one million, eight hundred thousand dollars, were truly more or less incidental in the final decision of Gordie Howe to come out of well-earned retirement and put on skates again after 29 years with the Detroit Red Wings of the established N.H.L.

There were those who felt "the greatest of them all" was a traitor to the N.H.L., selling his loyalty and deserting to the new rival W.H.A. for a pile of Texas greenbacks. Some Detroit area sports fans were hurt that their own Gordie would forsake his adopted hometown. To them, Gordie Howe was more than a superb athlete, he was an institution that belonged in Detroit as much as the General Motors Building. To think that some Texas outriders had galloped into town and had thrown a lasso made of dollar bills . . . why that was unforgivable!

There were others who knew that Howe was no traitor, who knew most of the whole story. Howe, being the quiet, gentle guy that he is off the ice, did not make much noise over the shabby treatment he had been given by the Wings' front office. He had even been isolated from his former teammates.

That management of the Red Wings, most of whom were also long gone within a year or two, had destroyed the allegiance he might have felt under different circumstances.

N.H.L. President Clarence Campbell understood. He said as much to Gordie in a private conversation after the move to the W.H.A. had been announced. He said, "Gordie, I guess we took you too much for granted!"

The big attraction that the Houston Aeros and the W.H.A. held for Gordie was the realization, as Colleen had said, of the long-cherished dream of playing professionally side-by-side with his teen-age sons Marty and Mark.

The intense desire for family togetherness on the major league ice grew from a March of Dimes charity exhibition in 1966, a game that drew capacity attendance to Detroit's Olympia Stadium to watch the "Howe line" for the first time: superstar Gordie, flanked by Marty and Mark, then 11 and 10 years old, respectively. The youngsters had been playing hockey almost as long as they could remember, moving up the ladder from one junior team to another as fast as their ages and skills progressed.

It was "only an exhibition" game to the fans who had turned out for the sake of charity and to savor the sentiment of the Howe line, but this single experience firmly planted in the mind of Gordie Howe the seed of the dream.

It was on September 7, 1971, at age 43, pain-wracked by continuing arthritis in both wrists and other injuries suffered through 25 long major league seasons, that Gordie officially hung up his skates.

With almost every National Hockey League record to his credit, including the mark for longevity, Howe was bone-weary; the joints and the muscles ached as injuries from long ago took their toll. He was tired and in pain.

The Detroit Red Wings were on a downhill slide, plagued by front office troubles that spread their poison like an octopus's tentacles into the newspaper stories and columns and on radio and television and to the fans, the customers who were now staying away from Olympia Stadium and, most importantly, among the players.

Hockey, Red Wings style, was no longer fun. On the scoreboards the Wings were losers. Too often the post-game press queries were about the latest front office hassle, about the coach who had just been fired, or about the new coach who hadn't yet put the Wings on the winning trail, or about the coach who was rumored to be on his way out, or the latest unpopular trade of a talented and long-time team-mate.

Also, on a personal note, there was no way Gordie could foresee the fulfillment of his dream of the "Howe line," at least under the then existing regulations of the N.H.L. Players must be at least 20 years old, although Gordie was only 18 when he came up to the N.H.L. from the minor league. Further, there was no assurance, in fact little likelihood that other N.H.L. teams would permit the Detroit club to draft and retain the younger Howes when they were ready.

It seemed obvious that the selfish interests of the rival team owners would prevail at that time. After all, what owner wouldn't want the services of a talented youngster, especially when he wore on his playing uniform the family name that had assured box office appeal and publicity value for more than two decades. The appeal of box office dollars was likely to be victorious over sentiment.

Regardless, it would be five more years before second son, Mark, was 20. Gordie Howe knew he couldn't suffer through five additional years on the slim hope that he would then have a year or two as teammate with his sons.

With nothing to gain by staying active, Gordie announced his retirement and accepted a job with the Red Wings' front office. That, too, turned sour—but more on the Red Wings' "mushroom treatment" later.

In the quarter century as an active major league player on the Detroit Red Wings team, Gordie Howe established new records in every possible way. In the later years, every time he skated onto the ice he set a new mark—every time he shot a goal, every time he assisted with a goal. He had won just about every award that was available, some of them many times.

Two that he missed were rookie-of-the-year honors for the 1946-47 season, and the Lady Byng trophy any year, awarded annually to the most gentlemanly player in the N.H.L.

It seems certain that Gordie would have been tremendously embarrassed if his name had ever been linked, even so casually, with that award. Not that Gordie was the most penalized player in the N.H.L., but there are many of his former competitors who insist he should have been.

A powerfully built man, Howe has been rated as one of the most aggressive, most physical players in N.H.L. history, but a man so clever when committing bodily mayhem that he was seldom caught at it, at least percentagewise.

Justice would seem to have been done, however, because Gordie still ranks second in career penalty minutes, behind his former teammate on the famous Red Wings "production line," Ted Lindsay. Second in penalty minutes, but well down the list of most penalized. Several players averaged two minutes or more penalty per game played. In fact, Lindsay's average was 1.8 minutes per game. Howe's record was a whisker under one penalty minute per game for the 1,687 games he played in the N.H.L.

Gordie Howe's style of very physical play had a major purpose—to intimidate the opposition. Being guaranteed they were going to be clobbered by this six-foot, 200-pound freight train on skates, there was a tendency to back off a bit.

2

Born on the Farm

Superstardom did not come easy for Gordie Howe, although he made it look easy. In fact, a careful review of his life reveals that nothing has really come easy for the Canadian lad from Saskatoon.

He was born—or at least gifted at an early age—with the desire to succeed, and he was also gifted with a natural talent as a skater and hockey player; but the talent had to be developed and refined and honed to the fine edge, and he never stopped trying from the first moment that he strapped on his one skate. Yes, that is correct, Gordie Howe had only one skate at the beginning.

Gordon Howe was born March 31, 1928 in the small community of Floral, Saskatchewan, Canada, the third son and the sixth of nine children, four boys and five girls, born into the midst of Depression-era poverty.

Although their town lay in the heart of Canada's wheat-farming country, Albert "Ab" Howe decided to give up the farm, which was not paying off, and move his young and growing family into nearby Saskatoon, where he operated a small auto repair garage, later worked on construction projects, and eventually retired as the superintendent of maintenance for the city of Saskatoon. In between there was much hard work and, especially during those early Depression years, some hard times, made easier by the warm family love that marked the Howe home through the years.

The original move from Floral was made when Gordie was just nine days old. In spite of his 31 years of constant traveling throughout the United States and Canada, and more recently to Russia, Gordie has known only three home towns—Saskatoon for sixteen years, the Detroit area for twenty-nine years, and Houston for two years plus.

Floral, Gordie's birthplace, was once described by the *New York Times* as a granary on the grim high plains of Saskatchewan, settled by homesteaders somewhere out between Saskatoon and futility.

Saskatoon was described as a town founded by a temperance society. By the time the Howes moved there in 1928, the Depression was ruining homesteaders and collapsing the local potash industry.

Ab Howe had gone up to Canada from Minnesota under the Homestead Act, which granted land to anyone willing to work it, but when he wasn't able to grow much of anything, he took a job as a mechanic in a gasoline filling station.

The senior Howe, now 79, was always tall, thick, and strong, and an indomitable worker. The heritage to Gordie is quite apparent.

Gordie has been told that his father was "so broke he couldn't afford the shells for his shotgun so he'd run down coyotes and kill them with his bare hands to collect the bounty. He used to kill gophers down in their holes for a one-cent bounty."

Gordie does not personally remember the Depression

hard times, "because as far as money is concerned, my father was a city employee as long as I can remember. He was a foreman for a long time. Before I was born he ran the farm and things got real tough there.

"My Dad was pretty good with horsemanship. He was a good horseman—a great horseman, matter of fact, and what he did was ride along beside the coyote, lean way over in the saddle and grab the back leg of the coyote. He had a knife and he'd hit it with one slash so the coyote couldn't get a bite at him. He'd slash a tendon in the leg to slow the thing down, then he'd jump off the horse, find a board or a fence post and crack it on the head two or three times and then take it home and skin it out.

"At that time they'd pay $12 or $15 for a pelt. If it was a big one, the bounty would look pretty good so then he had enough money to go invest in some shells and he'd be back in business again."

Ab Howe worked at many hard labor jobs during those miserable Depression years, not the easiest being on construction gangs. The period as an auto mechanic caused some physical problems when Ab contracted rheumatic fever working in the cold, damp repair and grease pits.

That was before the installation of automatic hoists to lift the automobiles off the floor, over the heads of the mechanics. The garage service pits of that era were literally that, deep holes in the ground; the car to be serviced or repaired was driven into position, straddling the hole in the ground.

Mrs. Katherine Schultz Howe was born in Stuttgart, Germany. She emigrated to Canada with her family and worked as a domestic until she met and married Ab Howe, then proceeded to raise the large family with tender, loving care, yet with the strength from her German heritage.

Gordie was the sixth of nine children, right in the middle, the third son. It is quite apparent that Gordie, in his own quiet way, was pleased that he was able to improve their way of life after he became a professional athlete.

He speaks proudly of his father, strong and determined, and remembers his mother as "the strongest woman I have ever known." A woman of great courage and stamina, she gave birth to three of her children without any help while her husband was working in the fields.

"When she felt the labor pains of the baby coming on, she would pull the water from the well and boil it. Then she would lay down, give birth, then cut the cord by herself and get up, all the while Dad was out in the fields."

Remembering the illness that took her life in 1971 at age 76, Gordie said her physician never would tell him the details of her illness because his mother wanted it that way. "We did have some good days," he said happily and proudly, and a bit sadly. For a few moments, as he said this, Gordie seemed to be completely wrapped in distant memories, pleasant and private memories of those young years in Saskatoon.

Mrs. Howe was a pale, gentle woman who talked softly, a sensitive lady, usually quiet, a woman devoted to her children and obviously proud of the accolades that came their way.

Mrs. Howe always tried to arrange her visits to Gordie's family in Detroit to coincide with the Red Wings' home games at Olympia Stadium because, as she said, "In Saskatoon we see only about four Red Wings games a season on television. One week the game comes out of Toronto and the next week it comes from Montreal, so it depends on the schedule.

"Every time I go to a hockey game I make up my mind I'm going to be calm, but then things happen and I'm up and down, and before too long I get so warm I have to get out of my coat. I just wish we could see more of Gordie on TV down home," she said during one of her Detroit visits.

Contrasting with his generally quiet wife, Ab Howe, a strong and proud man, always seems to enjoy conversation and is not above becoming involved in active discussions. He seldom hesitates to state his opinions, sometimes quite bluntly, always forcefully.

The day after Gordie Howe shot his 545th N.H.L. goal, on November 10, 1963, to become the greatest hockey goal scorer of all time, a newsman called the senior Mr. Howe for his comment. "What took him so long?" was the proud but blunt response.

3

The Schoolboy Discovers Hockey

As with so many things in this world of ours, the route into major league hockey is somewhat different today than it was 20, 30, and 40 years ago.

Now, players come into the N.H.L. and the W.H.A. from Europe in some cases, and for the Canadian and American youngsters there is more organized and more formal training for those who seem destined for the major leagues.

Until recent years, before the advent of the W.H.A., most of the N.H.L. regulars had similar backgrounds, the majority coming from Canada—some from the cities, but most from rural Canada, where hockey has been the king sport since the 1800s, an outgrowth of field hockey, which has been popular in England for centuries.

In rural Canada, where the freeze comes early in the fall, youngsters skate from the age of four and five on countless frozen ponds and lakes.

In Gordie's day, there were school hockey teams and community junior hockey teams, but nothing as organized as Little League baseball. Far from it.

In 1964, *Sports Illustrated* described Saskatoon as "a friendly town whose small boys dream of a kind of violence found not in dark alleys, but on the gleaming ice rinks.

"The slap of the hockey sticks and pucks is an ambient sound, and near every patch of ice parents stand shouting and encouraging and hoping and silently worrying about another stitch being added to a clean, young face."

It was in this environment that Gordie Howe traveled through boyhood, so no wonder hockey became a dominating influence in his life. For many Canadian youngsters, hockey was not only the way of life, but it could be the means of escape to a more financially rewarding world, the means to sports stardom and all the rewards that accompany such status.

Young Gordie Howe enjoyed those same dreams of future big-time N.H.L. combat, but it is doubtful that he ever thought of hockey as a way of escape. Although the Howe family operated on a tight budget during those trying years, there was an abundance of love in that family and life was enjoyable. Actually, when the time finally came for young Gordie to leave home he was a reluctant traveler.

In those Depression days, the family funds of many did not stretch far enough to permit a balanced diet at all times and the table at the Ab Howes was no exception.

Often oatmeal was the only food day after day, and young Gordie developed a calcium deficiency at one point; he had to take vitamins and suspend himself from the open doorways to strengthen his young bones.

As a youth, he was clumsy and half-coordinated. He became tremendously introverted and quiet and extremely shy, but mightily determined nonetheless.

Hockey fans today, not to mention his former teammates and competitors, can hardly believe that this seeming-

The Schoolboy Discovers Hockey

ly ageless superstar was once clumsy, awkward, and only half-coordinated.

As for being introverted and shy, those traits remain most obvious off the ice, even today. It is almost as if there are two different Gordie Howes.

At home or in public, away from the competition in the arenas, Gordie is an extremely gentle man, very devoted to his family: his wife Colleen, sons Marty, Mark, and Murray, and daughter Cathy.

In 1933, when Gordie was five years old, his mother quite accidentally started him on the long trail to professional hockey superstar status.

"I remember his first skates," she told the *Detroit News'* Bill Brennan back in 1966 when Saskatoon hosted a tremendous welcome home testimonial for their traveling hero.

"It was during the Depression," Mrs. Howe continued, "and a woman brought a grain sack full of clothes and things to our door, offering to sell them for a dollar." The neighbor needed the money and the Howes could use the clothes. That's the way they cooperated in Saskatoon in those dark Depression years.

"I believe I traded her a dollar's worth of milk tickets for the sack." (The story of the first pair of skates has been reported many times over the years and the price for the sack of clothes has floated from 50 cents to $1.50.)

"All the children were around so we dumped the bag of things on the floor and out fell a pair of ice skates. The skates skidded across the floor. "Gordie made a dive for one, yelling, 'They're mine!' His sister Edna was after them, too, so they each got one skate.

"Gordie had 'bobs' skates before, the runners that strap on, but these were regular shoe skates, a man's size six, and the kids had to stuff papers and rags into the shoes before they could get them to stay on their feet.

"They would go off every day, each with a skate on one foot and they'd each come back with the other foot soaked." A week went by before Gordie could swing a deal with his sister. In fact, he had to float the loan of a nickel from Mom to close the deal.

"When Gordie first tried to skate with both of them on, he was happy but exhausted. A couple years later I traded a package of his father's cigarettes for the next pair of skates for Gordie. A man had brought them to the door."

Those two vignettes point up so graphically the very tight money situation in Saskatoon in those Depression days, yet the tender consideration, the family love, and the cooperation among neighbors made it all so bearable, and, for the children, even fun.

Hockey became the overriding consideration in the young Canadian's life. Young Howe made the oversize skate shoes fit by wearing four and five pairs of woolen socks, then he wrapped newspapers around his legs in lieu of shin guards, and to protect against the bone-chilling winds.

"I guess the coldest it got in Saskatoon was 50 below," Gordie recalled later. "A lot of times it would be 25 below. It would be so cold that if you stuck your head out of the door at night the air was so crisp you could hear a guy walking two blocks away.

"Later, when I played goalie, I remember I used to skate a mile from my house to the rink, holding the pads up in front of me to cut the wind. At one rink, they had a heated shack. When a guy would ring a cowbell, the forward lines and the defense for the two teams would go off and sit in the shack by the potbellied stove and warm up while the alternates played. When we would change places, the guys in the shack would have to ask, 'Who's winning?'"

Even though the family had moved into town from the wheat farm, it was still wide open country and the youngsters could skate from their house out to the little airport, over five miles, with only the railroad tracks to cross.

When he wasn't in school or doing the family chores,

The Schoolboy Discovers Hockey

young Gordie was skating from early morning until well after dark, constantly practicing and learning maneuvering on skates, quick changes. He practiced stick handling with tennis balls, which froze all too quickly.

"There was a family named Adams in Saskatoon that had a rink with side boards between their house and the barn. We'd go all day there, about 15 guys on a side and play with a tennis ball in place of a puck. When the ball got frozen, we'd knock on her window and the lady would put our ball in the oven and throw out a fresh one for us."

Young Howe was so continuously occupied with hockey that he even practiced in the summer, when there was no ice. Once, he was shooting in his yard, off a piece of cardboard, aiming at a barrel with the shingled house for a backstop. When his father came home from work that day there were so many shingles all over the ground that his father called an abrupt halt to that activity.

In fact, that was one time young Gordie felt the sting of the strap a few times on his own backstop. "I had to do it," his father said later, "because we were only renting the house."

"A breakfast of oatmeal could last you practically all day," Gordie explained years later, "if you didn't want to take out time to eat lunch. We would skate down the icy ruts in the road to the rink. Sometimes there would be a whole flock of guys who would go home to lunch with me and my mother would have newspapers down on the floor in the kitchen so we could keep our skates on while eating, and she'd give us a stew or a thick soup. We'd even do that again for supper if we were going to skate again after dark.

"A lot of families had skating rinks in their own yards. With the first two or three snowfalls, we would build up the banks for the rink and then when the snow melted, it would run off the banks and freeze into a rink. Every school and playground also had a skating rink. There were rinks all over the town.

"When the chinook, a warm wind, would come, the

water from accumulated snow and ice would run into the lower areas, too, and we'd be able to skate as far as seven miles." At age 12, Howe was the star player on five different kids' teams simultaneously.

The intense interest in hockey spilled over also when the youngster was at home. "When I was a kid, if you sent a label from Bee Hive corn syrup to Toronto, they'd mail you back a picture of a hockey player. All of us kids would go up and down the alleys looking in the ash cans for the labels."

It is not surprising that Gordie was the champion of his town in that department, also. "I had about 100 pictures and when I pasted them in the scrapbook, along with a lot of autographs, it busted the seams."

He also had his hockey heroes. "When I played Peewee hockey our team was named the Red Wings and they'd give you a stick, your socks, a sweater and the name and number of a Detroit player. I drew Syd Howe, although we are not related, and so I wrote to him for an autographed picture. Later, when I came up to the Red Wings myself, Syd Howe was still there, in fact the Wings' leading scorer."

Gordie Howe never did get a chance to play as a teammate with Syd Howe, because Gordie was sent first to the minor league club in Omaha, and by the time Gordie became a Red Wings major leaguer the following year, Syd had retired. Syd Howe later was voted into the N.H.L. Hall of Fame.

One of Gordie's first hockey heroes was Ab Welsh, a forward with the Saskatoon Quakers. "I used to hang around the arena and watch them practice and he'd give me a stick that had lost its life, was a little logy. Then on the last day of one season, a redheaded defenseman for the Flin Flon Bombers gave me his old elbow pads." Little things like that continually whetted his desire to continue with hockey.

The center for the Flin Flon Bombers, when Gordie was the kid who used to help carry the skates into the Saskatoon Arena, was a young man named Sid Abel.

The Schoolboy Discovers Hockey

Nine years after that time, Gordie Howe, now a professional in the N.H.L., joined Sid Abel on one of the forward lines for the Detroit Red Wings; years later, he played under Sid Abel, who became coach and then general manager. Those were the more pleasant years in the big time.

It was during the 1947-48 season that the Red Wings assembled a forward line made up of Gordie Howe at right wing, Sid Abel in the center and Ted Lindsay at left wing, and the memorable "production line" led the Detroit team to the fabulous record of eight league titles, including seven in a row, and four Stanley Cup championships. Little could either Abel or Howe imagine, in those days when the Flin Flon Bombers would play in Saskatoon Arena, that they were both headed for the N.H.L. Hall of Fame.

Mrs. Bert Hodges was the manager of the King George Athletic Club's midget team when Gordie signed up, and she later recalled, "Gordie was always out there after dark. He knew what he wanted and he got it. It could be the coldest night of the year, but Gordie would be out there practicing all by himself."

He had to practice to overcome the clumsiness that plagued Gordie Howe, the boy, a trait that is long gone into history.

"Gordie was always such a big, awkward kid," Ab Howe was saying a dozen or so years ago. "He was always so much bigger than the others, and always very shy. I can recall his brother Vic always yelling at him, 'Gordie, when are you going to learn to stand on your own two feet?'

"Hockey was the only thing in his life," Ab went on as he chatted with *Sports Illustrated* writer Mark Kram. "Any time of the year, any time of the day, you'd see him with a stick in his hand. He'd walk along swatting at clumps of dirt or stones.

"The first time he tried to join one of the small teams here they sent him home because he wasn't dressed properly or something and I was hopping mad. Ever since then I've always told him to never take any dirt from nobody, because if you do, they'll keep throwing it in on you. That's the way life is. He's learned it all right."

Gordie's mother, normally quiet and reserved, was angry when some of the youngsters nicknamed her son "doughhead" because he was so quiet, big, and clumsy.

"That means stupid," she said, "or someone who doesn't know anything, and Gordie was never stupid. It used to bother him, too, but he'd never fight with the kids because he was so much bigger than most of them and he was always aware of that advantage."

Gordie's gentle, inhibited nature caused him problems in school, because he wouldn't burden the teachers with his problems. He completed the eight grades of elementary school, but ten years were required to get the job done.

As his mother recalled, "He always tried, but the second time he failed the third grade it took the heart right out of him. I remember seeing him coming down the street crying. 'Is the work too difficult?' I asked him. 'Don't you understand the teacher? Do you ask her questions about what you don't understand?'

" 'No, Ma, I don't want to bother her.' Then we both had a good long cry."

Never a brilliant scholar, he suffered from the knowledge that he was lacking in that department. As a boy, embarrassed by his failures in school, he was driven more and more into reclusion. Although withdrawn, he became more determined to make a success of his life, to strive further. When he started playing professional hockey he made use of those periods of free time while traveling to work crossword puzzles as a means of improving his vocabulary.

The shyness and the inhibitions remained for a long, long time. Even today, although Gordie is called upon for hundreds of radio and TV interviews, the introversion is very apparent. When signing autographs, which he has done more

The Schoolboy Discovers Hockey

than 100,000 times, Gordie still has the "Aw shucks, not me" look. He is willing, but just a bit embarrassed by all the attention. He may be Gordie Howe, superstar, the greatest of them all, to his fans, but to Gordie he is still that young fellow from the Saskatoon plains.

Ab Howe recalled an incident involving the teen-age Gordie when they were working on a construction job together one very hot Canadian summer day.

"At the end of the day, one of the workers suggested we go get a nice cold beer and I said, 'Sure,' and suggested to Gordie, 'Here, Son, go get yourself some ice cream and soda.'

"Later on, we come back and there's Gordie sitting on the curb with the money in his hand and he explained, 'Aw, Dad, I didn't want to go in there with all those people.'

"Once, later on, a girl was chasing him while he was playing baseball here during the off season (during his earliest N.H.L. years). So they were parked one night out in front of the house and the girl is telling him how much she thinks of him. Gordie, I can just see him, is squirming and he finally says, 'Well, if you like me so much, why don't you let me get out of the darn car?' "

He may have been bashful, but he was strong as an ox. One summer, when Gordie was 16, he and his dad were at work on a construction job where three men struggled to get a boulder into a truck, but they couldn't budge it. Ab Howe waved them aside, called Gordie over and whispered, "Now don't let me down." The two Howes got the boulder into the truck with ease, so it appeared, but Gordie still insists that his father did most of the work.

"I used to work at construction jobs to build myself up. It was a kind of weight-lifting program I didn't know I had, but I was doing it basically to get stronger in the arms and the back, but it would kill me today," he added with a laugh. "I used to work my butt to the bone handling concrete all day."

4

Painful Early Views of the Outside World

Gordie Howe and the Detroit Red Wings seemed destined for each other from a very early point in young Howe's boyhood, and a long trail of circumstances, now history, bears that out.

The Detroit hockey team had been admitted to the National Hockey League in 1926, two years before Gordie's birth in Floral, Saskatchewan, when a group of Detroit men headed by Charles Hughes purchased the Victoria Cougars (and retained the Cougars name, for a while).

After a disastrous first season, 1926-27, the Cougars owners were desperate, having lost close to one hundred thousand dollars at the gate as well as enough games to land them in the N.H.L. cellar, so they were ready—more than ready—when N.H.L. President Frank Calder suggested they talk with the now retired N.H.L. great John James Adams, who had just finished helping Dave Gill coach and manage the Ottawa Senators to the Stanley Cup championship.

Sportsman-businessman Hughes could hardly disagree when Jack Adams walked into his Detroit office and laid it on the line—"You need me more than I need you!" Jack Adams was to play a very important part in the hockey world of Gordie Howe.

As the family of Ab Howe was battling its way through the great Depression after the 1929 stock market crash, so was the Detroit hockey club fighting for its continued existence. Just as it was during the industrial inflation-recession upset of 1974-75, the Motor City was badly hurt by the failing economy and increasing unemployment of the 1930s. The team's name was changed from the Cougars to the Falcons, but that didn't help much at the box office or on the scoreboard. On the road, the Falcons traveled by day coach and their meals were more often cheese sandwiches served wrapped in wax paper.

Under Jack Adams' guidance, the Falcons won in their division in the 1933-34 season, then went on to the Stanley Cup competition, where they lost four straight to the Chicago Black Hawks, the same season that Gordie Howe was finding his first skate in a Depression-era bag of clothes purchased for 50 cents or a dollar.

As Gordie learned to skate and handle a hockey stick, the Falcons tobogganed back to the N.H.L. cellar in 1934-35.

In April of 1935, just a few days after Gordie's seventh birthday, another important move for the future of Gordie Howe was taking place in Detroit—the purchase of the almost bankrupt hockey club by James D. Norris, Sr., a Chicago millionaire and hockey buff from years back.

"We'll call this team the Wings," Norris announced on his first visit to Olympia Stadium. He had once played on a team in Montreal named the Winged Wheelers. "In fact," Norris continued, "we'll call it the Red Wings and our emblem will be a winged wheel, which ought to sit good with Henry Ford and the Detroit car people."

Painful Early Views of the Outside World 27

Norris's first player purchase, at the urging of Jack Adams, was Syd Howe from the St. Louis Fliers for the huge sum, for its time, of $35,000. In that first season, 1935-36, the Detroit Red Wings won their divisional championship and went on to skate all over Toronto three games to one to win their first Stanley Cup, the first of seven, all under the management of Jack Adams.

That Gordie Howe and the Red Wings were destined for each other is clear if you remember Gordie's recollection that his team in the Peewee league was named the Red Wings, and that he drew the name and number of Syd Howe.

Gordie first came to the notice of the Red Wings when their scout, the late Fred Pinckney, came across the lanky, talented kid playing hockey on a Saskatoon school grounds rink when Howe was just 13 years old.

As his hockey skills developed, so did his muscular body, helped in no small measure by his work with his dad as a 14-year-old construction gang hand during the summer.

In the summer of 1943, when Gordie was 15, the Red Wings almost lost him. With so many able-bodied men off to service for World War II, the N.H.L. scouts were hurriedly seeking younger talent, younger than they normally would, and several had their sights set on Howe. It was Russ McCrory who was the most on the ball: he was the first scout to visit the two-story hockey-scarred shingled house on Avenue I North in Saskatchewan in 1943, for a talk with the Howe family. McCrory was working for the New York Rangers, and he was pursuasive as they sat in the parlor.

Gordie sat quietly and listened intently as the visitor from Manhattan explained the Rangers' tryout proposal to Mr. and Mrs. Ab Howe, and finally the deal was consummated, a deal that was to lead Gordie to a very brief and very unpleasant introduction to major league hockey and to the world outside of Saskatchewan.

Later that summer, Ab and Katherine Howe saw young Gordie aboard a sleeper for the overnight rail journey to

Winnipeg. When he got off the train he asked directions to the Marlborough Hotel, where he learned he was to room with another major league hopeful, a would-be goalie.

All they did those tryout days was to walk from the Marlborough to the old Amphitheatre for practice and evaluation, then back to the hotel at night. That was just as well, because young Gordie was not much for exploring a community. Complicated route directions scared him.

Later, during his early years in Detroit, he solved that dilemma by learning the routes to everywhere from the Olympia Stadium. No matter where he was in town, or where he was going next, he would always go back to the Olympia to start the new journey. He would never cut from one location across town to another. Always back to the Olympia and start fresh.

His first day at the New York Rangers' tryout camp was a disaster. He had never seen any truly professional hockey gear, so when the trainer gave him the pads and protectors he didn't have any idea how to put them on. The young rookie dumped all the equipment on the floor in front of him as he sat on the bench; he looked around the dressing room and watched what the other guys did, then followed suit.

Gordie was not stupid, by any stretch of the imagination, but he was too bashful and introverted to ask for help. He was so overly considerate of other people that he felt he would be imposing on them if he sought their assistance.

It is a well-known fact that teen-age boys, in an attempt to disguise their own embarrassment in a strange environment, will sieze any opportunity to kid another youngster, sometimes being unintentionally mean in the ridicule. That is what happened in the Rangers' rookie dressing room. The other kids noticed Gordie's delaying tactics, realized his confusion, and then teased him about it. He was ready to flee back to Saskatoon.

It has been written that the Rangers' men blew the opportunity of signing the rookie who was destined to become the star of stars in the N.H.L. and later the W.H.A., but that is an unfair and inaccurate reflection on their judgment. Gordie stuck it out for a week at the Marlborough and Amphitheatre sites, even though his would-be goalie roommate was dropped after three days. At week's end, when Lester Patrick and Frank Boucher called the homesick Howe up to their room at the hotel, to sign him, he just shook his head and said, "Thanks." He told them he was too lonesome and just wanted to go back home to Saskatoon.

"The Rangers wanted me to go to Notre Dame school, which was in Saskatchewan and I thought it might be a pretty good idea, but I wanted to go back home and be with my friends, so I didn't sign any card.

"The one thing I have regretted is that I didn't go beyond the eighth grade, elementary school, and the Notre Dame school would have been good for me. However, I have obtained a pretty good education traveling so much, and I always have read a lot.

"If I had gone to Notre Dame, as they wanted, I would probably have been Ranger property. Once you sign an A card, or a B or a C card, you are more or less tied to them. As it was, I went home, still a free agent."

Once again, that pre-ordained Detroit Red Wings-Gordie Howe quarter century relationship.

Back home, Gordie put aside any thoughts of the big time in the N.H.L. and went about finishing his eighth-grade elementary school education, but he still demonstrated his love for hockey by an all-consuming devotion to the sport, whether in practice or in games.

Many Canadian youngsters took up hockey as a means of escape from the rural and small-time Canadian way of life, but it becomes apparent that this was not Gordie's reasoning or planning. If he was looking for an escape, he would have seized the Rangers opportunity. Neither would he have been so slow to accept the Red Wings offer that came the following year.

In 1944, Fred Pinckney, the Detroit Red Wings scout

who had first looked over the youngster three years previously, now watched with more than a little interest as young Howe played in a Lions Club hockey league in Saskatoon. Later Pinckney sat in that same parlor, explaining to Ab and Katherine Howe the Detroit hockey philosophy, as Gordie sat quietly and listened intently.

The Red Wings tryout camp offer was genuine, but the youngster was still hesitant. This trip to Windsor, Ontario, just across the river from Detroit, was three times as long as last year. Saskatoon to Winnipeg was just about 500 miles. The journey to Windsor, about 1,600.

Young Gordie wanted to go, he did want to play major league hockey, but the memory of last year's pangs of loneliness frightened him. The wise and crafty father sensed the turmoil in his son's mind and he moved quickly with just the right touch of impatience.

Ab Howe recalled later, "He wasn't too swift about making up his mind and I had work to do."

But Gordie broke into the conversation with, "No, I wasn't because I didn't know what the heck was going on, to tell you the truth, because I had two outfits around me, the New York Rangers and the Red Wings."

The elder Howe replied, "The man [Pinckney] laid out all the details, but Gordie was pretty slow at signing, so when there wasn't much more to be said, I got up and told Gordie that I had to finish hanging the kitchen door and I said, 'If you want to play hockey, this is your chance. If you don't want to, say so. I have to hang a door!'"

Young Gordie Howe signed with the Detroit Red Wings, to go to their tryout camp. "I had asked Mr. Pinckney if I knew anybody that was going and he said, 'Yes, a whole car full.' There were 22 of us in that sleeper. It took two days and two nights."

This time, a little more effort was needed for the long train ride, so Pinckney, recognizing a great N.H.L. prospect, bought the kid a new suit and a pair of shoes. He stuck a $5 bill in Gordie's pocket along with the railroad ticket. Young Gordie Howe was on his way to Windsor, Ontario, just across the Detroit River and almost in sight of Olympia Stadium, the beginning of the greatest professional hockey career of all time.

To clear up an often-printed error, Gordie Howe remains proud of his Canadian heritage, and while he loves and appreciates his adopted country, Gordie Howe has remained, and always will, a citizen of Canada, working in the United States on a permanent visa.

Red Wings coach and general manager Jack Adams was impressed with the big, rangy youngster who skated so easily and always seemed perfectly balanced, so Adams called the rookie over to the boards and asked, "What is your name, son?"

Adams, later recalling the incident, commented, "A lot of kids that age choke up when they start talking to you, but this one looked me right in the eye and said, real easy like, 'My name's Howe, but I'm no relation to that Howe over there,' and he pointed to Syd Howe, one of our leading scorers. I remember saying, 'If you practice hard enough and try hard enough maybe you'll be as good some day.' "

The practice and tryouts continued at Windsor for the better part of two weeks. The tryout experience at Windsor Arena was a little more palatable for the Canadian rookie than had been the case at Winnipeg the previous summer, but he was still a loner, bashful and homesick in spite of his direct response to Jack Adams that first day. Adams did not recognize the bashfulness until the end of the tryout camp, when he officially signed the youngster.

Because of N.H.L. age requirements, the Detroit club had to send young Howe to an amateur team with which they were affiliated, one located at Galt, Ontario, about 160 miles northeast of Windsor. Adams gave the kid a $500 bonus and agreed to pay him $1,700 annually starting the following year, when he would be with the farm club.

"After we signed Howe," Adams recalled, "he walked out in the hall. Later on, I came out and there he was looking kind of glum. 'All right, Gordie, what's the trouble?' I asked, 'Something bothering you?' He replied, 'Well, you promised me a Red Wings jacket and I don't have it yet.'

"I felt like telling him, 'You want a hundred of them, go get a hundred of them.' He was some kid. When he was 16, he was the best prospect I ever saw. When he was 17, he was the best pro rookie I ever saw. When he was 22, he was the best young major leaguer around and later, well he's the best hockey player anyone anywhere has ever seen."

The season at Galt was not a completely happy one for young Howe, who missed his home and family and friends back in comfortable Saskatoon. As for hockey, it was more a case of marking time, because at 16 he was too young to play in regular season games, so he practiced regularly with the team and played in the exhibition games.

At the start, the Galt team management, trying to be helpful, enrolled Gordie in the local high school, but when he walked to the big brick building and saw all the students gathered outside, the old fears grabbed him, so he continued along the railroad tracks instead and landed a job as a spot welder with Galt Metal Industries. Gordie had told them about his experience on construction gangs back home, but neglected to admit that he had never before done any welding. What they assumed, they assumed, and he quickly learned by watching.

As had been promised, Jack Adams dispatched young Howe to the Omaha club in the United States Hockey League, and he quickly showed his skill as a player. During the 1945-46 season, he scored 22 goals and had 26 assists, earning 48 points for Omaha.

For the 17-year-old, however, it was a bit more difficult adjusting to his new life as a professional athlete, adjusting to the activity that seems normal to the travel-wise veterans.

In his first swing around the league, the players were in

a Minneapolis hotel, relaxing before heading for the stadium and the regular night game. About 4:30 in the afternoon, young Howe went downstairs, planning to eat dinner.

"Several of the guys were there in the restaurant," he recalled later, "but I looked at that big dining room and it looked so nice that I didn't want to go in, so I went around the corner and I had a milk shake." Certainly not much fortification for a rugged game of hockey, but it obviously didn't slow the kid down, because "I scored two goals on that milk shake and we beat them three to one."

Quite a contrast with the seasoned pro. For a night game, veteran Gordie's dinner was set about 3 P.M., usually steak, peas, lettuce, fruit gelatin, and tea. After dinner, he would lie down for a two-hour nap. For an afternoon game, "I just played on my breakfast eggs," he says, with a chuckle.

5

Debut at Olympia

Detroit hockey fans were introduced to the self-conscious rookie at the start of the 1946-47 season, and while coach Jack Adams labeled him a "sure-fire star," he was not overly impressive on the ice, still in the learning process. However, few players ever hit the league with better physical equipment. Faithful in his conditioning, Gordie scaled 187 pounds then. (A dozen years later he was a little heavier, just 204 pounds on his just-over-six-foot frame.)

The first goal as an N.H.L. major leaguer came on October 16, 1946, and Gordie will never forget it. "It was in our opening game at Olympia, against Toronto. The puck was lying loose ten feet from the net and I just slapped it in. I kept the puck and took it home and gave it to the folks, but I have no idea where it is now. The trouble with those things is that they lose their importance in later years."

Not many games later, Gordie learned another valuable lesson, the need to hit the puck hard when shooting for a goal. "The cardinal sin," he said, "is to slide it easy. There was a game in Boston when I had Frank Brimsek beat, but I just slid the puck toward the goal. Brimsek came over with his lumber and got a piece of the puck. Sid Abel was playing then and he said, 'Any time you see that net, drill it.' I went back and beat Brimsek again, in that same game, and really let the puck go. I never forgot it."

At first, Howe was a fighter on the ice, doing battle with any opponent who got in the way. Coach Adams tolerated this for a while. Eventually, he called Gordie into his office for a private conference. "What are you trying to do, beat up the entire N.H.L. one at a time? Look, kid, you've proved you can fight, now prove you can play hockey!"

There was a reason for Howe's penchant for scrapping during his early Red Wings days. "When I was with Omaha the year before," he recalled with a chuckle, "I had said that when I skated out on the ice I hated every other man out there. Yes, that's the right word, I said I hated them.

"Well that statement went right up to the Red Wings and they said I had the right attitude and that I would be with that club—the Red Wings—the next season.

"I just figured if that was the way I had made it up from Omaha to the Wings, then that must be the way they wanted me to play and that was the way I was going to play.

"It was shortly after that that Jack Adams took me to one side and told me to prove I could play hockey as well as fight."

Gordie played in 58 games during his rookie season with the Detroit Red Wings, 1946-47, and scored 7 goals and came up with 15 assists, for 22 points, certainly no record-breaking performance.

Neither was it a record-breaking season for the Red Wings. They finished fourth in their division and were eliminated early in the playoffs.

Over a span of 21 years, the Detroit Cougars/Falcons/Red Wings had compiled a so-so record. Four times

Debut at Olympia

they had won their divisional title and three times they had won the coveted Stanley Cup, but in six other years they had not even qualified for the playoffs. In all fairness, those Depression years had hurt the Detroit hockey club probably worse than most others because of the special vulnerability of the auto industry to poor economic conditions, but that was past history.

Better days were just around the corner. Perhaps it was because of a more seasoned Gordie Howe, or perhaps because of a new coach, or both.

Jack Adams was still the general manager, but young Tommy Ivan was installed as coach. Ivanoff was the full name, but he has been known simply as Tommy Ivan throughout his great N.H.L. career.

Ivan was a little fellow compared with most hockey players in the N.H.L., about five feet, five inches, but a fellow who could move easily and quickly. He had played amateur hockey at Brantford, Ontario, until he was hit in the face by a puck.

Those pucks travel about 125 miles an hour, when propelled by an expert.

With his playing days now behind him, young Ivan decided to remain in the sport and in Brantford, so he started coaching a kids' team there.

Later, the Detroit club signed him as coach of their junior teams in Guelph and Galt, both in Ontario, until World War II came along and he joined the Canadian Army.

After the war, he was back with the Red Wings and their farm club in Omaha, the year that Gordie Howe was at Omaha. The next year, as Howe moved up to Detroit, Ivan was sent to the Indianapolis Capitals in the American League, before he himself moved up to the Red Wings.

Adams, a big, blustery take-charge guy, couldn't completely let go of the coaching reins. What coach has been able to refrain from second-guessing after he moved out of that slot to be the big boss?

Adams and his wife sat in the stands just one row behind the bench at every game, and he seldom refrained from offering advice to the coach.

Regardless, they both must have been doing something right. Just look at the record.

From the 1947-48 season through 1953-54, the Red Wings won six straight N.H.L. championships and three Stanley Cups, and it all began with the formation of the famous "production line" of Gordie Howe, Sid Abel, and Ted Lindsay.

For Ivan's first season on the job, the Wings finished second and were going good in the playoffs until they lost in the finals. The production line was on its way!

When Gordie was called up to the Wings from Omaha, he slept most of the first few nights in a storage room in the basement of Olympia Stadium, as one way of saving his meager funds, keeping a hockey stick alongside the bunk for use in whacking the occasional rats.

Even though a rookie, he was clever enough to choose the No. 9 when it was available, because that would get him a lower berth on the trains.

As that first season began, Gordie joined some of the other Detroit players at Ma Shaw's rooming house near Olympia, and soon he became very close to Ted Lindsay, his teammate, roommate, and close friend.

Actually, it took young Howe three full years before he matured into a top-flight hockey player. First, it was the constant fighting, which manager/coach Jack Adams corrected, and then perhaps it was lack of confidence, because he was still the young farm boy from Saskatoon, transplanted into the great industrial Motor City and into the major league, but still among strangers.

Young Howe had tremendous strength, and he was a skillful skater and stick handler, but it still took a while for him to put it all together.

After three seasons, 1946 through the spring of 1949,

Debut at Olympia 39

Gordie had scored only 35 goals, playing in 158 games, but there were other experts who joined Jack Adams' original prediction that this young man was a future hockey great.

Each of those 35 goals gave the youngster a great feeling and, wearing a big smile, No. 9 would flash by the net with his stick raised straight up toward the ceiling in the traditional goal sign.

With the great forward line of Howe, Abel, and Lindsay starting to click, the Wings had won their divisional championship in that 1948-49 season, but they lost in the finals of the Stanley Cup playoffs. Little did they realize that this was the first of six great championship years, one of the greatest records in the N.H.L.

6

On the Edge of Death

The 1949-50 season was to be a great one, yet bittersweet, for 21-year-old Gordie Howe and the 23-year-old Detroit Red Wings, Howe having his best major league season, the production line moving rapidly, and the Wings en route to their divisional championship and the coveted Stanley Cup.

In this season, Gordie Howe was again named to the N.H.L. All-Star second team at right wing, same as last year, which had been his first such honor. Before his playing career ended, Gordie would be chosen for the N.H.L. All-Star teams no fewer than 21 times, a league record, and he also would hold the record of being selected for the All-Star teams in 15 consecutive years. After the N.H.L., Gordie was also destined to win All-Star selection with the World Hockey Association.

In 1949-50, his forward linemates Ted Lindsay and Sid Abel were chosen for the All-Star first team, along with

Maurice "Rocket" Richard of Montreal. Ironically, although no one realized it at the time, one of Gordie Howe's All-Star forward linemates was Ted Kennedy of Toronto.

Disaster was to strike for Gordie, and Ted Kennedy would be the trigger man.

1949-50 was a great playing year for Gordie. The N.H.L. season had been lengthened, this year, from 60 to 70 games and Howe played in every one of them. He scored 35 goals and was credited with 33 assists for a regular season total of 68 points, two more than his first two years put together.

The Red Wings finished on top in the Eastern Division and went into the Stanley Cup playoffs with visions of success dancing before their eyes.

It was on the evening of March 28, 1950, just three days before Gordie's 22nd birthday, that the Wings were battling the Toronto Maple Leafs on their home ice at Olympia Stadium.

The Wings had fallen behind 4 to 0 and were battling to turn the tide. Howe, as always, was giving his all for the cause and he made a move to body-check Toronto's Ted Kennedy, his earlier All-Star teammate. Exactly what happened in that scramble has never been clearly defined.

Regardless, Howe crashed head first into the boards and collapsed in an unconscious heap directly in front of the stunned Red Wings bench. Kennedy's stick is said to have rammed Gordie dead center in his right eye, although Kennedy always denied that.

Immediately, the unconscious player was carried on a stretcher as the capacity crowd stood silent and stunned. It was that season that Gordie Howe began to have an electrifying effect on hockey fans everywhere, but especially those in Detroit. Howe was transported to a waiting ambulance always on standby at the rear door to Olympia.

From the Stadium, with siren wailing and red lights flashing, he was rushed to Harper Hospital. No one knew the extent of the injuries, because they were more internal than obvious, but everyone sensed that this was a very, very serious situation, as indeed it was.

It was soon ascertained that he had suffered a severe skull fracture and brain hemorrhage, as well as severe eye injury.

Dr. Frederic Schreiber is credited with saving Gordie's life by drilling into the head to relieve the terrible pressure from the brain hemorrhage. Obviously, his condition was critical.

Today, Gordie doesn't talk much about that crash into the boards, and he says, in fact, that he doesn't know what did happen, whether or not Kennedy's lumber hit his eye. He doesn't even remember hitting the boards.

Back in 1969, however, the *Reader's Digest* quoted Gordie as saying that he recovered consciousness just before Dr. Schreiber began the 90-minute operation to relieve the pressure on the brain. About the plan to drill into his head, Gordie is quoted as saying, "That got me a bit het up. I didn't know where they'd stop." It may have happened that way.

The midnight surgery completed, Gordie lay hovering between life and death for days, under an oxygen tent. Many felt that Gordie Howe would never play again. In fact, there was fear that he would permanently lose the sight in his right eye. Even Gordie worried about that as he lay recuperating many days later.

One evening, when he sensed that the nurses were not around, Gordie completely disregarded his doctor's orders and carefully removed the bandages that covered his entire face and head, almost like a mummy.

"I just wanted to make sure that I really could see," Gordie explained later with a sly grin. Of course, it is a matter of record that he did recover from the head and brain injury, and he did retain excellent vision, but the accident left him with a slight facial tic and, even today, the dark eyes blink often, without control.

When he returned to action, his teammates started to

kiddingly call him "Blinky" and he never resented it. In fact, he often used the expression himself, such as, "Old Blinky was flying tonight, eh?" or "Did you see Old Blinky miss that goal early in the game?"

Another thing happened to young Gordie Howe as a result of that accident. When he came back to play the next season, he was more aggressive. Perhaps he wanted to prove to the opposition that he would never let the frightening experience affect his play. Some opponents have called him the strongest, meanest, and toughest player in sport—any sport—and the frightening Stanley Cup playoff experience might have added that competitive spark.

While young Howe lay in his hospital bed, his teammates went on to win the playoffs and then took on the New York Rangers in a vigorous seven-game war. Moving into the right-wing spot in place of the ailing Howe was 24-year-old Gerry Couture, a five-year Red Wing veteran, also from Saskatoon.

Couture also had just enjoyed his best regular season, scoring 24 goals, so he fitted well with Lindsay and Abel as the series ground to a close, all tied up, three games each.

In the final game, with the Rangers leading, the 38-year-old Abel was visibly tiring, but with the time running out he managed to score the tying goal while on his knees, a valiant and successful effort.

In the 28th minute of the overtime period, 25-year-old Pete Babando came off the bench to score the winning goal. The Red Wings had won their fourth Stanley Cup, the first in seven years, but the injured Gordie Howe had been cheated out of the chance to play in his first. There would be others—in fact three more—in which he could star, plus two W.H.A. Avco Cup series.

7

Love Bowls Him Over

Miss Colleen Joffa, then a Detroit high school senior, first heard the name Gordie Howe in the spring of 1950, just two days before the young hockey star reached his 22nd birthday.

It was after the semi-final game of the play-offs for the Stanley Cup in which Gordie Howe was critically injured at Detroit's Olympia Stadium and rushed to Detroit's Harper Hospital. No matter where the accident occurred, it would have made sports page headlines, because young Howe had already captivated the enthusiasm of the fans and press with his accomplished style of play. Because the accident happened on the home ice, there was much additional breakfast table conversation in the Detroit area that next morning, and the Joffa household was no exception.

Young Colleen Joffa knew little about hockey—it held no interest for her at that time; but as she came down to breakfast that Wednesday morning, March 29, 1950, she found her father storming angry that this should have happened to the young Red Wings star.

Colleen, like a young girl with no interest in hockey, paid little attention, but she was later to remember the incident, after she had graduated and was working as a secretary who liked to bowl for recreation.

She was bowling in a league at Joe Evans' Lucky Strike Alleys on Grand River in Detroit, across from Northwestern High School and about three blocks from Olympia Stadium, and Gordie also was an occasional bowler on some of his free nights when the team was at home and there was no game scheduled.

Coach Tommy Ivan practiced the Wings early in the mornings on those off days, using the cunning theory that, "If you get them up early enough in the morning, they'll get to bed early enough at night." Not a bad idea at all.

It was on one of those free nights during the 1950-51 season that Gordie first noticed the stunning blonde bowler. Then he began to spend more and more time at the Lucky Strike lanes. Love at first sight was Gordie's lucky strike.

Always the bashful boy from the Canadian farm, Gordie fretted for many bowling nights as he tried to find some mutual friend who could introduce them. He didn't have the nerve to approach the girl directly. It had to be done properly, as he had been taught back in his growing-up years.

After a handful of weeks, young Howe convinced the bowling alley proprietor to do the introductory honors. Joe Evans introduced Colleen to Gordie Howe and Gordie's companion that night, Vic Stasiuk, a new Red Wings left wing who had come over from the Chicago Black Hawks.

Later in the evening, Evans nodded in the direction of the tall, slope-shouldered Howe and asked Colleen, "How did you like meeting that celebrity?" "Is that a celebrity?" she asked the stunned Evans, who quickly responded, "Are you kidding?! That's Gordie Howe of the Red Wings!"

For a moment, it still did not register with Colleen, until

she recalled that morning several months earlier. If her father thought so much of Gordie Howe, he must be okay.

The first date was a little delayed, however, because Gordie was still the bashful one. In fact, some of his teammates and competitors kiddingly referred to him as the "bashful basher," recognizing the two views of Howe, the one off the ice and the one at work on skates.

The first few "dates" consisted of three-hour phone conversations until Gordie's courage matured and then on his first date he took Colleen to meet his teammate, roommate, and close buddy Ted Lindsay.

Years later, Colleen recalled that first date quite tenderly. "Ted Lindsay was 'family' to Gordie, really the only family he had outside of Saskatoon."

From that point they dated when they could, but it is obvious that the life style of a professional athlete is not really conducive to romance, especially with a working girl. There are the too frequent and too extended out of town trips, then when the team is at home, practice in the morning, games at night, with the most time off being in the afternoon.

Also, from the beginning, Gordie had a feeling for the fans and was among the most accommodating of all athletes. Tired as he might be, Gordie would never disappoint the fans, standing for a long time outside the Olympia exit to sign autographs and talk, as long as the customers wanted to talk.

The romance continued to blossom through two and a half seasons as Colleen Joffa became a hockey fan in her own right.

After four seasons as a major leaguer, Gordie Howe had come into his own. He had matured as a man and as a player. The terrible crash into the boards had not slowed him even the slightest; apparently it had made him more forceful. Each game, each week, each month, each season he improved.

It was on February 17, 1951, that Gordie scored his

100th goal, in a game at Montreal. That season, the Wings again led the Eastern Division to the championship, but they lost in the playoff semi-finals. Howe's record, playing the entire 70 games, was 43 goals and 43 assists for 86 points.

For the 1951-52 season, Gordie again played in all 70 games and scored a phenomenal 47 goals and 39 assists, for 86 points. He was voted the Most Valuable Player in the league, winning the Hart Trophy, the first of six he was to earn.

The award for the Most Valuable Player was donated in 1923 by Dr. David A. Hart, father of Cecil Hart, a former coach-manager of the Montreal Canadiens. The winner is selected annually by vote of the hockey writers and broadcasters in the N.H.L. cities.

The Red Wings again won the divisional championship and went on to win the playoffs and then defeat Montreal four games to zip to capture their fifth Stanley Cup. In the third game, which they won 3 goals to 0, Gordie Howe scored two and assisted Ted Lindsay on the other one.

As the Howe-Joffa romance burst into full bloom and the happy twosome looked forward to marriage, Gordie recorded another great season, 1952-53, scoring his 200th goal on February 15, 1953, against the Black Hawks, playing in Chicago.

For the regular season, Gordie again played every game, increasing his production to 49 goals, 46 assists, and 95 points. Again he was voted the Most Valuable Player, taking home his second Hart Trophy replica.

The Wings again won their Eastern Division championship, but tumbled in the playoffs for the Stanley Cup. Regardless, Howe was given a boost in salary to what was then, for the N.H.L., a magnificent sum, $15,000 a year.

April 15, 1953, two weeks and a day after his 25th birthday, Gordie Howe and Colleen Joffa were married at Calvary Presbyterian Church overlooking Grand River, with Red Wings Ted Lindsay, Reggie Sinclair, and Marty

Pavelich attending, and Mrs. Pat Lindsay, wife of Gordie's closest friend, the matron of honor.

More than 22 years of marriage have produced a very obviously happy family, with four children: Marty Gordon Howe, now 21 years old, named for Gordie's former teammate Marty Pavelich; Mark Steven Howe, now 20; their sister Cathy, now 15, named in part for her grandmother; and Murray, another future hockey player, now 14, named after a one-time Red Wing player, Murray Oliver.

The marriage also produced a partnership that has really worked, with Colleen not only the bookkeeper but also the family and business manager, scheduler, and the one who has to say, "No, thanks," to the hundreds upon hundreds of requests of all kinds that come Gordie's way.

While the three boys each had the urge to play hockey at very early ages, the idea was never suggested or encouraged by the parents. Neither was it discouraged. They just let nature take its course.

The low-key attitude around home is illustrated by a couple of Colleen's family anecdotes. When Marty was of kindergarten age he answered the telephone one day and the conversation went like this:

"Is your father there?"

"No, sir."

"Is he at work?"

"No, sir. My father doesn't work. He plays hockey."

Later, when Marty attended elementary school, he came home the first day, quite indignant, and challenged his mother with, "Why didn't you tell me that Dad is a famous hockey player?"

As Colleen recalled, "To us it was just an everyday situation that Gord was a hockey star. At home, with the family, with Marty and Mark then, he was just a person, a special person, yes, but not because of his hockey ability."

The boys developed their interest in hockey early in life. They liked to accompany Dad to the practice sessions when his schedule would permit, and from the time they were about seven years old they were playing on "bantam" and "squirt" division teams, a bit more organized—for better or worse—than during Gordie's growing-up days in Saskatoon. The early teams were in the Detroit Division of Parks and Recreation Leagues.

Cathy enjoys skating, but has not indicated any special interest in skating professionally in any sense. When she was six and seven years old, she was taking lessons at the Detroit Skating Club in ballet and figure skating, but without any serious intent.

Fortunately, Colleen Howe is a natural organizer, telling the children in the morning what sort of a family schedule was ahead and what was expected of them. In those earlier years she would get breakfast for the children and get them off to school, then prepare a second breakfast for Gordie and herself, when he was at home. Next the children would be home for lunch; that would be followed by Gordie's early dinner, before his afternoon nap, to get ready for the game. With Gordie on his way, the family dinner followed.

With all that, Colleen organized and managed the various activities in which Gordie became involved as his sports stardom increased. In addition, she has always been involved in civic affairs and she was business manager for various junior hockey teams, not only running their operations, but raising money through candy sales and ticket campaigns.

Through all the hectic business activities, the family always stood out as most important.

"We learned early to accept the fact that Gord would be away much of the time, so we cherished his time at home. We tried to arrange to have free evenings, plan the meals together, because the children had so much they wanted to ask him.

"Gord was always very good about spending time with

the children. As they were growing up, his away games which were televised became family affairs. The children would put on their pajamas and all snuggle up in front of the television set. Usually the two smallest, Cathy and Murray, would fall asleep before the end of the game, but when Gord came home, Marty and Mark had many questions to ask: 'What really happened on that play? What was the fuss all about? What about the penalty, it sure didn't look that way on television.' "

As the boys began to understand the technicalities of the game, Gordie could explain and interpret, which obviously laid the background for the professional skills that Marty and Mark have recently demonstrated.

In their junior hockey days, Marty and Mark were each playing 60 games a year, young Murray was playing 45, and Gordie was playing 70 games, 35 at home, 35 away, plus practice sessions, and somehow or other Colleen Howe managed to keep them all coordinated and each headed in the right direction at the proper times.

In 1971, Colleen was honored as the United Fund Sportswoman-of-the-Year and in 1974 the family was honored at the annual Detroit-Windsor Freedom Festival as the international family of the year, and this was even after he had left Detroit to work and play in Houston, Texas.

The Freedom Award they received put them in the same ranks with President John F. Kennedy, Arthur Goldberg, Lowell Thomas, Prime Minister Lester Pearson, and the American Astronauts, previous winners.

The award, the presenters said, was because the family "symbolized the spirit of the Freedom Festival through their enthusiasm and zest for living and their dedication to community service."

Young Marty, asked to speak, said, "I really had nothing to do with winning this award. All I did here was play football, skate, and play hockey."

8

Through His Admirers' Eyes

Early in the 1953-54 season, when Red Wings coach Tommy Ivan was asked to spell out the factors that made Gordie Howe such an accomplished hockey player, he had to fumble for the right words.

"The best I can do is to go outside hockey and compare him with Stan Musial, the baseball player," Ivan replied. "Nothing flashy. No trouble. Hardly a peep out of him. No new angles for you newspapermen to write about.

"Like Stan Musial, all Howe does is to lead the league year after year and knock the opposition's brains out for you, especially when you need the big one. He's just the best hockey player I ever saw."

At age 24, he had scored his 200th career goal in N.H.L. competition, against the very tough Chicago Black Hawks, 200 goals in seven years of play. In the 1952-53 season, Howe had been on his way to scoring 50 goals to tie the record then held by the great Maurice "Rocket" Richard, but he was stopped at 49, mostly because of his own generosity in passing the puck to other players for the final blow into the net.

Wings general manager Jack Adams first noticed that tendency to be generous in the 1951-52 season, when Howe seemed headed for Richard's goal-scoring record. "I told Ivan to use Howe a lot in our last few games, but Gordie kept passing the puck to Sid Abel. Finally, Tommy asked Howe what in hell was he up to.

"Howe drawled in his slow, laconic way, 'Oh, Ol' Boot has a bonus coming for getting 20 goals this year, y'know,' using Abel's nickname, 'Bootnose.' 'If he's in front of the net, I'm going to give him the puck.' "

They both missed their marks that year: Abel got only 17 goals and Howe was stopped at 47. The following year he would get to 49 at the end of the season, the highest total he ever reached. It was one of the few records he never owned.

In the two decades since those years, goal-scoring has been recorded at higher levels, partly because of the additional games in the season, 78 now, plus the expansion of the N.H.L., which introduced less accomplished players, at least less experienced players, who presented a weaker defense for such great ones as Phil Esposito and Bobby Orr of the Boston Bruins, and Bobby Hull of the N.H.L. Chicago Black Hawks and now of the Winnipeg Jets of the World Hockey Association.

In the N.H.L., Phil Esposito scored 76 goals in 1970-71, playing 78 games, and the following year he accounted for 66 tallies, while Bobby Hull scored 58 goals playing for the Black Hawks in the 1968-69 season, 76 games.

This past season, 1974-75, Hull, now with the Winnipeg Jets, was going for an all-time major league hockey record of an average of a goal per game, at least 78 for the 78-game season. He did not quite make it.

Red Wings manager-coach Jack Adams had watched the mild-mannered but tough 18-year-old rookie score his first major league goal on October 16, 1946, off Toronto's

Turk Broda, with assists by veteran Sid Abel and Adam Brown. Howe also lost two teeth in that first N.H.L. regular season game.

Seven seasons later, Adams was still the general manager of the Wings, with Tommy Ivan as the coach, and the robust, outspoken Adams still found it easy to define the greatness of the player he called "my guy."

"Howe is big, at six feet, 196 pounds. He's the cleverest stick handler in the game. He shoots well with either hand, the only ambidextrous shooter in the league. He's one of the surest skaters on the ice [an observation that was to be confirmed later by experts, especially 21 years later as the "old man" was a member of the Houston Aeros and Team Canada playing against the Russian All-Stars].

"Howe is so aggressive," Adams continued, "that nobody ever rides him off a play. No big man before him ever had all that. By the time Howe reaches 30 years of age he will be known as the greatest hockey player anyone anywhere has ever seen!"

Even Adams could not foresee that in his late 40s, Gordie Howe would still be playing and proclaimed the Most Valuable Player in the World Hockey Association, or that he would be scoring continually to post a record that probably never will be equalled, more than 2,000 career points. There is no one even close.

Coach Ivan's estimation, back there in 1953, continued: "He's just coming into the hockey player's peak age period—25 to 28—and I figure he will last another five or six years as a forward. After that he can put in several good years as a defense man."

Hah! Another "five or six years?" More like two decades, as it developed!

Ivan's estimation was based on more than the muscular body that Howe had developed as a school boy, then enhanced as a 14-year-old hand on a Saskatchewan construction gang.

"He takes scrupulously good care of himself," Ivan

pointed out. "He still doesn't smoke or drink. The last time we were in New York with a night off, in a hotel just a few steps off the 'great white way,' he was in bed at 9:45."

Other expert watchers have noted that Howe always displayed the energy-conserving ease of an exceptionally natural athlete. In 1952 he was breaking 70 in golf, and had never taken a lesson. He learned by watching. During the summer he was batting .370 in Canadian semi-pro baseball, and he often liked to work out with the Detroit Tigers baseball team just for fun and to keep in shape. He likes deep-sea fishing in the summer, for relaxation and recreation. Howe cannot stand being idle, and he is attracted to other sports as if there was a magnet there.

He safely negotiated the longest ski run at Aspen, Colorado, the first time he wore skis, and explained, casually, "I try to do anything well so I won't make a darn fool of myself." That old inferiority complex from the old Depression days, still showing through once in a while.

Also, his skating style was deceptive to the point that he suckered many an opposition player. He skated and maneuvered so easily that even his friends accused him of loafing, but it just looked that way. Ivan commented: "His long skating stride and his terrifically quick reflexes make even the hard ones look simple"—and here, again, Ivan went outside to another sport for a comparison—"like Joe DiMaggio coasting in under a tough fly ball."

Big, barrel-chested Jack Adams was a tough man and he admired young Howe for his ability as a hockey player. At one time, talking about the many young players who had started with him, he said with a chuckle, exaggerating considerably, "Those boys were so young when they came to the Wings that when I came home from a road trip, those who hadn't gone would rush up to me yelling, 'Daddy! Daddy! What did you bring me?' "

His feelings about young Howe were expressed this way: "I'm a strong admirer of Rocket Richard, but for pure versatility, high purpose, and team contribution, my guy is the greatest."

For 16-year-old Gordie Howe, walking into the Red Wings tryout camp, a scared young lad from Saskatoon, his first meeting with tough Jack Adams had been a pleasant one, and the impression stuck. Adams was impressed with Howe as a player, while Howe transferred some of his loneliness to Adams as a sort of substitute father figure.

It all came to the surface in 1966 when Jack Adams was presented with the first annual Lester Patrick trophy as the man who had done the most for hockey in the United States, named in honor of the great coach of the New York Rangers, a pioneer in hockey.

The presentation took place at Toots Shor's banquet room in New York and Jack Adams' "my guy," Gordie Howe, was there. In typical Howe grace and brevity, for he never has liked to speak at a microphone, he said, very quietly and very seriously, "Close to my father, up very close, it's you."

Adams was caught up in a melancholy thought about the passing time as he rose to give thanks to Gordie and the others: "May God take all of you in his arms, but not too soon."

The following year, at the comparatively young age of 38, the second winner of the Lester Patrick trophy was Gordie Howe.

Two years after the first presentation to Jack Adams, the great general manager and coach of the Red Wings was dead, May 2, 1968, at age 72.

9

The Meanest?

Professional hockey is a rough, often brutal, contact sport. In hockey, the experts will tell you, as in war, the best defense is a good offense, and Gordie Howe proved early to his competitors that he is tough. It was a self-protection device. "If you can be shoved around, why, you're going to be shoved right out of the league," he explained.

Those competitors who slugged, slashed, and tripped Howe usually got it back, doubled in spades. "You do something to him," one enemy said, "and he won't even let on that he noticed it, but after the next scramble, you've got a few stitches to prove that he really did notice."

Once a veteran defenseman had checked Howe too forcibly—at least Howe thought so—and soon the rival player painfully discovered that his nose had been broken by a surprisingly swift attack from the Howe elbow, "and I was the one who got the penalty," he lamented later, grudgingly and admiringly.

Howe, in his low-key way, seems to indicate that much of the history about him has been overplayed. He denies the often heard description from the opposition—their claims over and over—that his moves with the high stick and the elbows are so swift and devious that they often escape censure by the officials.

"I don't know where they get that idea," Gordie said recently. "I agree that I have spent a lot of time in the penalty box, but I don't feel that I play rough or that I get away with it. I know they do say that, but I still don't see where they get that idea."

Gordie Howe is not the most penalized hockey player in the record book. His one-time teammate and good buddy Ted Lindsay holds that dubious honor. Lindsay, with 17 seasons and 1,068 games behind him, was penalized a grand total of 1,808 minutes, to top everyone in the history of the N.H.L.

Our own bashful basher, however, is in second place in the accounting of total minutes spent in the N.H.L.'s version of durance vile, 1,643 penalty minutes over a span of 25 seasons and 1,687 games. Quick arithmetic shows that on a per-game basis Ted Lindsay was naughty many more times, or at least he was caught at it more often.

They might be considered an odd pair of playmakers, the six-feet-tall Howe and the five-feet-eight Lindsay—Howe usually mild-mannered and Lindsay ever combative. Roommates before their weddings, they might be labeled the original odd couple, buddies on the ice and off the ice until two decades later when Lindsay became an N.H.L. television sportscaster and Howe moved to the rival W.H.A. The long friendship broke apart when Lindsay made some on-the-air disparaging comments.

Back in happier days, the 1952-53 Red Wings team had some crackerjack players. Terry Sawchuk was leading N.H.L. goalies with an average of only 2.02 goals against him. Five of the Wings were in the list of ten top scorers in the league that year, Gordie leading the league for three straight years, and the others were Lindsay, Red Kelly, Alex Delvecchio, and Metro Prystai.

Howe and Lindsay had been playing the forward line together for seven seasons. Their longtime teammate, Sid Abel, was gone to be player-coach for the Chicago Black Hawks and Delvecchio was fitting in between them very nicely.

It was the long-time familiarity that Howe and Lindsay had with each other that provided the distinct hockey advantage. "I don't even have to take the trouble to look around for him much of the time," Gordie explained at that time. "Where I happen to be with the puck at any given moment tells me where Lindsay is."

As one writer quipped, at any given moment the contentiously cussing Lindsay was likely to be wrist-deep in a fight, with the innocent-faced Howe alongside him or skating up fast.

Lindsay seemed to love the fighting and his penalty totals proved that. Howe always seemed to enjoy his good-looking roommate's talent for scrapping. "He really cleaned that Richard's clock for him last night," Gordie chortled to friends one morning.

Howe was more mild-mannered and he often said the best part of hockey was skating. "After a day's practice when we're not playing that night, I like to go out to a public rink at night and skate some more," he said. What about those occasional fights on the ice? Apparently the price of a great hockey reputation, because Gordie explained, a grin across that innocent face, "They look me up."

Because of Howe's aggressiveness, the defense against Howe was often as fruitless as trying to contain a quart of water in a pint jar. Following a collision, Howe was invariably the one who got up first. Rival teams didn't really play him, they merely endured him. It was his tremendous drive, his desire. One teammate explained, "Gordie has simply got to be first. If you take the puck away from him, even in practice, he'll always come right after you and get it back."

Howe's calm demeanor is amazing, even in the midst of a furious battle. One night in the late moments of a tied game, he drifted through the entire Chicago Black Hawks team, controlling the puck as if it were taped to his lumber, right to the goal area, where he toyed with the rubber, the Detroit fans screaming for a goal, Jack Adams on the bench screaming for him to shoot.

As the opposing goalie made a dive for the puck, the cool and calm Howe spun on his skates and nonchalantly drove in the game-winning goal.

"What the devil were you waiting for?" demanded the irate Adams. "Shucks, Jack, I knew I had him but I wanted him to make the move. I just wanted to make sure."

It has been said here, earlier, that there are two Gordie Howes—quiet, unassuming, and bashful off the ice and aggressive and competitive on the ice. Perhaps that on-the-ice Howe should be, again, split in two—the mild-mannered, smiling, innocent-faced Howe, the clean-cut All-Canadian-American boy whom the fans learned early to adore. Then there is the guy who excels with his elbows as weapons, a man who, his opponents say, is skilled with the illegal high stick and so devious that the officials often fail to see the offense.

Howe denies that hockey is as rough as some people claim, especially when compared with professional football. "In football," he claims, "they are face to face with the same guy all through the game and they do whatever tricks they can to beat the guy, whether it's legal or illegal." Joe Schmidt, the great Hall-of-Famer of the Detroit Lions, once told Howe of an incident when he was suffering from a dislocated shoulder and was wired with a chain from around the biceps to the chest, to restrain the movement of his arm.

An opposing player noticed the chain and would grab it

and render Schmidt almost helpless. Between the halves, Schmidt had the trainer rig some barbed wire into the chain, and on the next play the opposing player was sent screaming and bleeding.

"Football players just delight in getting back at the other guy because they are playing nose to nose so often," Howe said, trying to show the difference.

Then, practically contradicting his own argument, he went on, "Of course you get a little hostile on the ice, especially during a playoff series when you play against the same guy day after day for an extended period. There's a little bit of animosity there. Although today [1974-75] that seems to be missing, that animosity, because you don't face the same players as often. When we used to play each team 14 times during a season you faced one guy all year long and there was a feeling built up there."

Actually, the opposing players have always seemed to admire Howe's talent for dirty playing and getting away with it, even though they were the victims. His almost angelic "Who me?" expression fakes out the referee and the opponent shrugs.

The offensive attack is a defensive move, a hit-or-be-hit situation; frighten your competitors, let them know that if they hit you they'll get it back, doubled.

Jim Hunt of the *Toronto Star,* a long-time Howe observer, once described Gordie as "the most prolific scorer in the game's history, the smartest player, slickest stick handler, best playmaker and finest passer. Also, when the occasion calls for it, he's a mean man who will work over a rival with a stick or an elbow, a recognized master of the art of high-sticking."

One rival player once said, about Howe's use of his elbows: "Have you ever watched anyone trying to scrape the ice off a windshield? Well, that's Gordie Howe and those elbows." The elbows move so rapidly that the fouls are seldom seen by the officials. King Clancy of the Toronto

Maple Leafs once nicknamed Howe "The Wiper."

Ted Lindsay once admitted, "Gordie gets away with more than anyone in hockey." Toronto defenseman Allen Stanley tangled with Howe and came out of it with a broken nose, and Stanley was hit with the penalty, which is like pouring salt on an open wound.

Another time, Toronto's Carl Brewer fell in a tangle in back of the net, just as the play was stopped, and Brewer was on top. "Okay, Carl, the play's over," said Howe, and Brewer resisted the temptation to give him one more shot. In the next period, the same pair tangled again, with Howe on top. Brewer, feeling the ground rules had been established, relaxed, and *pow!*, Howe gave him one in the ribs.

"Unless a player keeps asserting himself," Gordie explains, by way of justification, "the other players take it as a sign of weakness and start to climb all over you."

While Howe was aggressive and rough, he never was really a fighter, but he earned the heavyweight title of the N.H.L. in 1959 in Madison Square Garden in a battle with Lou Fontinato of the Rangers.

There had been bad blood between them for some time. Fontinato had cut Howe's lip earlier, and there were other hassles before this particular Wings-Rangers game. In a tangle, Howe saw Fontinato coming to join the fray and he ducked Lou's first punch. It has been reported that Howe grabbed Fontinato's sweater with his left hand and landed one square on Lou's nose with his right, that big hamlike fist. Four stiches were required to close a cut under one of Howe's eyes, but Fontinato landed in the hospital with a nose that was badly misplaced all over his face.

The following week, when *Life* magazine ran a full-page photo of Fontinato in the hospital, his nose broken and his eyes swollen, opposite a photo of Howe in the dressing room, with his shirt off and muscles bulging and rippling, many people were shocked.

Howe felt it had been blown out of proportion, but it was his last major fight, although it did not slow him down as an aggressor.

Howe may be rough, but he's not vicious. When Montreal goalie Gump Worsley lay helpless on the ice after a sprawling attempt to save the puck and prevent the goal, the puck was loose in front of his face. Howe could have rifled a shot that would have scored a goal, but it would also have rearranged Worsley's facial features more than a little.

Howe dropped on the puck to stop the play and protect the rival goalie. "Thanks, pal," said Worsley. "Forget it," shrugged Howe. "I'll get other chances."

Several years later, Howe was asked about that incident and he just shrugged it away with, "It may have happened, but I don't remember it."

A few moments later, Howe apparently forgot the earlier disclaimer, as he said, seeming to apologize for being compassionate, "It was no big thing, although old Gump seemed to think so at the time."

When you sit with Gordie Howe in a restaurant, or in his home, watch his eyes light up as he assists one of his sons with a project such as rewinding some tangled fishing line on a reel, it is difficult to imagine—no, make that impossible to picture this man as a dirty, tough hockey player, but the record does speak for itself, and so do the observations of those men who have played against him through the years, even allowing for some competitive bias that might color their thinking.

Off the ice, this big, lumbering, muscular six-footer, who doesn't seem to have any shoulders, the arms growing right out of his thick neck, this big guy with the shy smile, is as unassuming and as considerate as any big-name athlete ever.

He has been favorably compared by many with Gary Cooper, the silent hero type, and his patience with the fans who seek his autographs is surprising. His reserve must be contagious, because fans will so often say the autograph is for a son, or a nephew, never for themselves.

"Why do they do that?" he asks, as those big eyes blink, the constant visible reminder of his near-fatal crash into the boards at Olympia Stadium.

10

Skills and Honors Escalate

In the thirteen-year span from the 1950-51 hockey season through 1962-63, Gordie Howe not only led the Red Wings; he led the entire National Hockey League in scoring six different years, and here is his amazing record, beginning with his rookie year:

Years	Games played	Goals	Assists	Points	Penalty minutes
1946-47	58	7	15	22	52
1947-48	60	16	28	44	63
1948-49	40	12	25	37	57
1949-50	70	35	33	68	69
1950-51	70	43*	43**	86*	74
1951-52	70	47*	39	86*	78
1952-53	70	49*	46*	95*	57
1953-54	70	33	48*	81*	109
1954-55	64	29	33	62	68
1955-56	70	38	41	79	100

MR. HOCKEY

Years	Games played	Goals	Assists	Points	Penalty minutes
1956-57	70	44*	45	89*	72
1957-58	64	33	44	77	40
1958-59	70	32	46	78	57
1959-60	70	28	45	73	46
1960-61	64	23	49	72	30
1961-62	70	33	44	77	54
1962-63	70	38*	48	86*	100
17 years	1120	540	672	1212	1026

* led the league.
** tied leading the league.

As mentioned earlier, the first three seasons were the ones needed to reach his maturity as a professional hockey man. The fourth season he was coming into his own but was seriously injured during the playoffs. After the injury, it was noticed by friend and foe, teammate and opponent, that he was much more aggressive.

Sparked by his new-found enthusiasm and with his skills now honed to a sharp edge, Howe led the league in goals scored with 43, and he tied as the league leader with 43 assists, but had the league point lead all to himself, a total of 86 for the season.

Quite coincidentally, the man who tied him with 43 assists for the season was Ted Kennedy of the Toronto Maple Leafs, the same one who triggered his critical injury.

Also, as mentioned earlier, in 1951-52 and 1953-54 Howe was reaching for 50 goals in one season, but his generosity in passing the puck to others cost him the privilege of tying the mark set in 1944-45 by the great Maurice "Rocket" Richard of the Montreal Canadiens. Howe never did score 50 goals in a season. Today, 50 goals is still an accomplishment, but not the greatest of feats, because of the expanded schedules and the weaker opposition provided by some expansion teams in both major

Skills and Honors Escalate 69

leagues, with more than a dozen players accomplishing this in N.H.L. and W.H.A. history.

Howe once said, "There are stronger players than I am. Take Bobby Hull [then of the N.H.L. Chicago Black Hawks]. Bobby has a stock farm near Belleville, Ontario, and when he goes back to the farm, he doesn't call the cows, he just goes out and carries them into the barn."

On the other hand, arch rival Bobby Hull said, about the same time, "There are 240 of us in the N.H.L. but Gordie Howe is in a league by himself."

Howe's response to such compliments in those days was, "I'm just a lucky old farm boy. To me, hockey's always been tremendous fun. Maybe that's what keeps me going."

One observer's description: "With his long, lean countenance, his lazy sort of walk and his laconic way of saying, 'Yep,' 'Nope,' or 'Goldarn!', he's the spittin' image of a bashful Gary Cooper."

Years ago, the *Reader's Digest* said: "A deceptively fast skater who takes loping, almost languid strides, he can rev up to a fantastic 40 feet per second without even seeming to try. But when he cruises in on the opponents' net-minder, Howe is at his facile best. Instead of cocking his stick and slapping the puck, he snaps off hockey's hardest shot with a mere flick of the massive wrists and the puck takes off at 120 miles an hour!"

St. Louis goalie Glenn Hall put it even more directly: "All you can do is turn and see if it's in the net."

In one sense, he is a strangely built man. The lines of his massive six-foot, 200-pound body are unusual, because he shows virtually no shoulders. The strong arms appear to grow right out of his thick neck, almost like branches from a strong oak tree, although they hang loosely at his side when he is standing or walking. When he is at work on the ice, those massive arms are flailing.

A teammate once quipped, "In a suit, Gordie is shaped like a bowling pin. When Gordie buys a new suit, the tailor has to leave the coat hanger in it so it won't look like a sack."

While his physique is a bit unusual, he looks like what he is, a powerful and agile athlete and just the kind of a man you'd like to have alongside when walking in any dark alley. With Gordie Howe on your side, never worry.

When he was running his hockey school in St. Clair Shores, Michigan, near Detroit, he told his young students, "A major league hockey player needs three things: one, ability to skate; two, knowledge of game; three, guts. If you haven't got all three you might as well take up another sport. And, of the three, I believe the last is the most important. Guts!"

A hockey puck travels about 120 or 125 mph and Howe told his students that if they started worrying about that eight-ounce piece of frozen rubber hitting them, there's no place in the game for them.

When Howe won the Hart trophy for the 1956-57 season as the Most Valuable Player in the N.H.L., his third Hart trophy in 11 seasons of play, it moved him into select company because he was then one of only three men who had earned the Hart award three times. Gordie had first won Most Valuable Player recognition back to back in 1951-52 and 1952-53. Now, after a span of four years, he was back again.

Howie Morenz of the Montreal Canadiens started his triple-play Hart record in the 1927-28 season, then repeated back to back in 1930-31 and 1931-32.

Eddie Shore, the great defensive ace of the Boston Bruins, came along with the Most Valuable Player honor the following season, 1932-33, and then repeated 1934-35, 1935-36 and 1937-38 to become the first four-time winner.

For Gordie, the honor was nice; but, probably more important for a young man raising a family, there was a $1,000 bonus that accompanied the trophy. This boosted the Howe seasonal bonus to $4,500. He had received $1,000

Skills and Honors Escalate 71

along with the Art Ross trophy as the league's leading scorer, with 44 goals, 45 assists, and a point total of 89. There was also a bonus of $1,000 as a member of the Eastern Division championship team, the Red Wings, plus a $500 bonus for getting into the semi-finals of the playoffs. The remaining $1,000 to make the $4,500 total came when he was selected on the N.H.L. All-Star team for the fifth time.

Howe continued his winning ways, but the N.H.L. salary scale wasn't too generous. There were only six teams in the league in those days—Detroit, Chicago, Boston, New York, Toronto, and Montreal—a closely knit owner group, but they played a 70-game schedule, quite rugged for such a totally physical sport.

As Gordie reflected later, "Here I was, at least they told me I was the star of stars in hockey, and I had to work at two extra jobs in the summer in order to support my family, and my next door neighbor, a salesman, had a boat and trailer and a summer place and he was always taking his family on short vacations. Every weekend he was off on another trip, but I had to stick around Detroit, except when we went on business trips."

At a Congressional hearing on professional sports in 1957, before a committee headed by Congressman Emanuel Celler, it was learned that N.H.L. salaries averaged only $9,000, not great even by 1957 standards.

One thing certain, the Detroit sports fans had shown him their appreciation when he became the first active player in any sport to be inducted into the Michigan Sports Hall of Fame. That was in 1957, after 11 years in action.

After all, he had been an All-Star five times, played on eight N.H.L. championship teams, been on the Stanley Cup winning team four times, was the N.H.L. scoring champ five times, and had all kinds of honors from publications like *Hockey News* and *Hockey Pictorial.*

By the time Gordie reached the end of the 1962-63 season, he was closing fast on the all-time hockey scoring record, then held by the great Rocket Richard, who had retired three years previously.

The income for the 35-year-old Detroit ace was a bit sweeter now, said to be about $28,000 in salary money, plus some $9,500 in bonus payment earned by being better than others. It was reported at the time that Toronto's Frank Mahovlich was earning twenty-five grand a year and the New York Rangers were said to be paying their excellent defense man Doug Harvey $27,500, and it was generally believed that Rocket Richard had been getting at least $30,000 a year when he retired three years earlier.

It still bugged Gordie that he wasn't able to put aside a nest egg for the future, raising a family of four children, and with the extra demands that are always made upon sports heroes. He was associated in a tool and die business with Detroit Tiger baseball star Al Kaline, and he had opened his first "Gordie Howe Hockeyland" skating rink and was working on the staff of the annual Red Wings hockey school at Olympia Stadium.

The Gordie Howe Hockeyland was a beautiful place on Harper, south of Masonic Boulevard in St. Clair Shores, Michigan, not far from Detroit—on the far east side. A quarter-million-dollar structure, the ice patch for skating was 188 feet by 83, and there were seats to accommodate 1,500 spectators.

In the summer he also traveled through Canada for one of the country's major retail establishments. But, as Gordie said, he had to work at those extra jobs during the summer in order to gain a financial foothold.

His 1962-63 bonus had been earned as follows: $1,500 came with the Hart trophy as the Most Valuable Player; another $1,500 came with the Art Ross trophy as the league's leading scorer; the Red Wings added $1,300 as a reward for that goal production, 38 goals and 48 assists; being selected an All-Star for the fourteenth time in 17 years had brought $2,000; and his share of the playoff money brought another $2,750.

Skills and Honors Escalate   73

That Hart trophy was an N.H.L. record that still stands, an unprecedented sixth time as the Most Valuable Player in the N.H.L.

In the balloting among the sportswriters in the six N.H.L. cities, Howe had earned 30 points toward the MVP award for his work in the first half of the season, but his blistering second half brought forth all the honors, 81 out of a possible 90 points, giving Howe a total of 111 points, more than double the 54 points that went to the runner-up, Chicago's Stan Mikita. During that second half, Howe had scored 25 goals with 29 assists in 35 games, rugged going for a 34-35-year-old fellow.

Hockey writer Jack Berry of the *Detroit Free Press* summed it up nicely when he wrote, "If Howe hadn't won the Hart Trophy it would have been the biggest upset since Harry Truman whipped Tom Dewey. The amazing part of it is that Howe is 35 years old, past the normal hockey retirement age, but has shown no signs of slowing down."

And, as we know now, Howe was still going strong at age 47. Fantastic!

In that 1963 news story, Jack Berry also noted that Howe had taken his family on a Florida vacation at the end of the rugged hockey season, and he added, "Maybe he is swimming in Ponce de Leon's Fountain of Youth at St. Augustine. If so, look out!"

As a boy in Saskatoon, Gordie had not noticed the absence of a lot of money, because that was a more or less standard condition then.

With his moves into hockey, his first year with Omaha and then on the road with the Red Wings, it quickly became obvious that the facilities back home could be improved, and as rapidly as he could he allocated some of his pay to improving and building and making a better physical way of life for the folks at home.

As a result, Gordie Howe was very conscious of the need to plan for the later years for his own young family.

11

"The Greatest of Them All!"

Beginning in 1963 there was a catchy, lively song heard frequently on Detroit radio stations. It had been written and recorded by a Canadian musical group and immediately became a big hit wherever major league professional hockey was played, and of course that breaks down to only six major cities, but the interest spread from coast to coast throughout Canada.

It was written in tribute to the slope-shouldered giant on skates who had become the Most Valuable Player in the N.H.L. for an unprecedented sixth time, with other honors already detailed within these covers.

The simple words, sung with rousing enthusiasm, said it all:

> *Gordie Howe is the greatest of them all;*
> *The greatest of them all, yes the greatest of them all;*

> *They can have their choice of all the rest;*
> *'Cause if you're a Howe fan, you've got the very best!*
> *Gordie Howe is the greatest of them all;*
> *The greatest of them all, yes the greatest of them all!*

Certainly not Pulitzer Prize material, but it spelled out the enthusiasm of the hockey fans—at least many hundreds of thousands of enthusiasts.

Howe had a great image in Detroit, of course, but in many other N.H.L. cities, some said he was the dirtiest player in the game.

Gordie's long-time teammate and friend, Alex Delvecchio—later coach in 1974 and now the coach and general manager of the Detroit Red Wings—summed it up this way: "Definitely some of those people in other cities thought Gordie was dirty. Elbows, you know he would never admit it, but he'd stick a lot of leather in the opposition's face. If you got Gordie really mad, he'd give you a little wood, but only if you got him mad. Yes, he was dirty, but in a clean sort of way.

"Ted Lindsay [another Howe/Delvecchio teammate] was the most aggressive, toughest man I ever played with. He was a little crude, but he wouldn't back away from anyone, and he was a terrific team man."

Not unlike Gordie Howe, Lindsay's personality changed on and off the ice. Delvecchio continued, "Lindsay was Mr. Goodie Two Shoes off the ice, but you put those skates on him and he didn't care who you were. This was even in practice, anything. He was out there to play hockey and stay in the National Hockey League and he fought to stay there."

About the rough stuff in hockey, Delvecchio never felt, he said, that a "club should go out there and just go out physically and forget the hockey, but then again, I'd like to have the fellows, if something does come up, and if someone gets smart with you, there's no reason—they can't kill you or anything—there's no reason not to just go right back at them.

"This is something we [the Red Wings] probably lacked the last couple years [after Howe left]. There was really no teamwork and no one to back up a guy in any of the scraps."

Talking about aggressive players, Delvecchio recalled Frank Mahovlich, whom the Red Wings played against when Frank was with the Toronto Maple Leafs, then later Frank was with the Red Wings for two and a half years, 1968 to 1970: "Frank's the type that somebody had to hit him to get him awake, but once you woke Frank up, he was murder on the ice.

"When Frank was with Toronto this is one of the things we noticed and we used to tell our defense or anybody, 'Don't hit Frank. Let him rest. Don't touch him.' Frank was content to skate up and down, but when somebody hit him, he was a different man. Then there was trouble."

In the Howe days, the Red Wings' forward lines were great on teamwork, Delvecchio recalled. "It's just a natural ability out there, with instant reflexes and responses. If you see a fellow in the clear and you think he can go further than you with the puck, you give him the puck.

"That's how I lasted 23 years. I had a big guy on right wing and I say just give him the puck. He'll get the job done, and Gordie did.

"I definitely enjoyed setting up goals for Gordie and others. Being a center ice man, you are supposed to be a passer, set up plays and get things done and it didn't matter to me if I scored the goal or someone else on my team.

"Playing with guys like Gordie, you give him the puck and then you'd watch him, the type of plays and maneuvers he would pull off and put it in the net. It was just pretty to watch."

Delvecchio explained how they could anticipate each other's moves on the ice during the fast play: "We talked to each other in between periods. You know, Gordie loved to be all over the ice and that was my job. Sid Abel [the coach] would say, 'You'll have to tell Gordie to stay on his own side of the ice.' Gordie would just shake his head and indicate, 'Not me. You know I've been up and down there all night.' Gordie was all over the ice. He was great."

Another student of Howe was his first coach, Jack Adams, who recalled, even after he, Adams, had been replaced by Sid Abel, "They used to call Gordie 'Power' on the club and in practice a lot of the young players would just look at him sort of dumbstruck. The one thing that always thrilled me about his game is the way he keeps doing the unexpected. You can never figure what he's up to and you always figure when he's on the ice he will tie the game or win it. He was always remarkable under pressure, yet in the dressing room, even before a big game, he was always just as cool as he was on the ice."

Jack Adams liked to point out, "I saw the famous Jack Dempsey and Gene Tunney long-count prize fight, and I've seen a lot of other exciting sports events in my days, but this guy Howe has given me the greatest thrills of all. He hasn't changed a bit since the first day I saw him and I hope he never does. He's one of the most natural and unselfish persons I know."

With the customers singing the musical praises of "the greatest of them all," the Red Wings' management was either impressed or embarrassed, because just before Labor Day, 1963, a couple of weeks before the new season was to open, the team manager and coach Sid Abel announced that Howe had signed his contract for the 18th season, and they were going to pay him a "substantial" increase in salary.

Knowledgeable insiders and outsiders figured that the "substantial" translated to $2,000 and that Howe would now earn $30,000 a year. Abel beamed as he said, "As the best player in the N.H.L., he deserves to be the highest paid, which we think it is." Club policy always precluded any official figure statements.

"The Greatest of Them All" 79

As it had been generally accepted around the league for some time that Maurice "Rocket" Richard was being paid $30,000 annually when he retired three years previously, that would make Abel's statement accurate.

The Wings opened the season on Saturday, September 7, 1963, with Gordie Howe just four goals away from tying the record established by Rocket Richard. Howe had ended the 1962-63 season with an even 540 goals to his credit, along with 672 assists, 1,212 points in a grand total of 1,120 N.H.L. games.

The Rocket had ended his playing career in the spring of 1960 with 544 goals, 421 assists, and 965 points in 978 games in 18 seasons. Now, Howe was going into his 18th season with only four goals to tie, five to set a new mark.

The pressure on Howe and his Detroit teammates was not unlike that which was on baseball's Hank Aaron as he approached the Babe Ruth home run record. The linemates passed up their own scoring chances many times, passing instead to Howe, trying to set up the goals for No. 9, but he continued to be frustrated. Even Howe was not playing the goal-producing game he knew so well. Can you imagine Howe with only three goals to his credit during the first 50 days of the new season?

The tying goal, number 544, came on the home ice of Olympia Stadium October 27, playing against the old club of the Rocket, the powerful Montreal Canadiens. The goal was shot in spite of the very rugged checking of Montreal's Gilles Tremblay, who helped hold Howe to only two shots on goal all night. The second shot was a good one, coming at 11 minutes and four seconds of the third period, with assists from Bill Gadsby and Bruce MacGregor. The goal was scored at the expense of goalie Gump Worsley. One is reminded of the time Howe saved Worsley's face from probable damage and Gordie responded to Worsley's proffered thanks with, "Forget it. I'll have other chances."

Howe never was much for honors and milestones, but he was very happy to see that one behind him. It had come just 17 years and 11 days after his first goal during his rookie year on October 16, 1946, playing in Olympia against the Toronto Maple Leafs. That first one came from assists by Sid Abel and Adam Brown and at the expense of goalie Turk Broda.

There were other milestone records:

Goal number 100, at Montreal, February 17, 1951.

Goal number 200, at Chicago, February 15, 1953.

Goal number 300, at home against Chicago, February 7, 1956.

Goal number 400, at Montreal, December 13, 1958.

Goal number 500, at New York, March 14, 1962.

After Howe tied the old record, the pressure stayed on even more as Gordie and the Wings moved to break the record. Two weeks of frustration went by with No. 9 remaining scoreless until Montreal came back to the Olympia November 10, 1963.

Manager-coach Sid Abel said, before the Montreal game, that he had a hunch this would be the night and Abel determined he was going to work Howe for the maximum time to help him get the record out of the way. By this time, the tension was so great everyone wanted it over and done with.

It came in the second period when the Red Wings were short-handed because Alex Faulkner was in the penalty box for high-sticking Montreal's Ralph Backstrom. Abel sent Howe and Billy McNeill out to kill the penalty.

McNeill got the puck deep in Detroit territory and broke with Howe on the left and Bill Gadsby on the right. Two Canadiens were back, Jacques Laperriere and Dave Balon, and Charlie Hodge was in the goal, substituting for the injured Gump Worsley.

McNeill carried the puck down the right side, cut over toward the middle and past the blue line, then passed to Howe. Gordie didn't wait: using the power in his wrist, he snapped a shot from inside the face-off circle, about 15 feet from the goal. Hodge hugged the goal post to his left, but he wasn't quick enough and the puck rifled in.

Bedlam broke loose and the ovation from the sellout crowd of 15,027 Howe fans went on and on for more than seven minutes, as goalie Hodge banged the goal post with disgust, then went to his bench to rest while the Detroiters whooped it up.

As it happened that night, the Red Wings won it 2 to 0 and goalie Terry Sawchuk had earned a mark of his own, tying the old George Hainsworth record of 94 shutouts, set when he retired as a goalie in 1937. Hainsworth had played for Toronto and Montreal.

Sawchuk was to later go on and set the all-time N.H.L. goalie shutout record at 103 in 20 seasons.

The puck was retrieved and given to Gordie to add to his trophies and keepsakes. "I'm glad it's over," he said.

Playing for Montreal that night at Olympia was Henri Richard, by 15 years the younger brother of the Rocket. Henri had earned the nickname of the Pocket Rocket. As the final buzzer sounded to give the Red Wings the victory, Henri Richard skated over to Gordie and stuck out his hand in congratulation.

Later, Maurice Richard agreed, "I knew he would get it. He's a great player. How about that, scoring both the 544th and 545th goals against my old team."

Richard insisted, however, that Howe's record-breaking goal should go in the record book with an asterisk, like Roger Maris's home run record in baseball, pointing out that Richard's total had been accomplished in 978 regular season games, while Gordie had needed 1,132 games to break the record.

"I missed 169 games because of injuries," Maurice explained. "If I hadn't been hurt so often I would have scored 100 more goals."

It is always thus with records and record-breaking in different eras and under different conditions. The arguments can go on and on without end. "Now, *if*. . . ."

The many backers of Rocket Richard as the greatest player are quick to point out that Richard scored 50 goals in a 50-game season, and the best Howe ever did was 49 goals in a 70-game season. On the other hand, Howe's record of assists for other people's goals is the greater. He has always been generous, giving the goal chances to his teammates.

Richard is credited with being the most exciting shotmaker in hockey, very dramatic. "He would come up on you with his eyes lit up like 200-watt bulbs," one goalie recalled. "You couldn't miss him because he was so dramatic."

Howe is rated more subtle, a smooth and calculating skater, in command of the pattern of the play, and he does it so easily that he almost looks like he is loafing.

In 1962-63, Howe was to get a $1,000 bonus if he scored 35 goals, plus $100 for every goal over that, yet three times he went to the scorekeepers and insisted that goals credited to him really came from teammates. He ended the year with 38 goals and $1,300, having given away $300 because of his own sense of honesty and fair play.

One of those times, when he purposely passed to a teammate who was getting a bonus for goal scoring, he was helping a player who needed one more for the bonus. Howe took the puck, rocketed down the ice, faked out the goalie, and passed to his friend, who shot the all-important goal.

Then Howe skated to the Red Wings' bench and with a big grin on his face, asked, "Anybody else looking for bonus money?"

Sid Abel said, "If Gordie has ever had a fault, it is his tendency not to shoot as much as we'd like. He'd rather pass off to someone else." This about the man who is, now, officially, the world's greatest scoring hockey player of all time.

Gordie has always said the records don't mean all that much to him, but he indicated differently, quite accidentally, one day early in 1975, while he was still playing for the Houston Aeros.

Bobby Hull, a friend and competitor on the W.H.A. Winnipeg Jets, was being interviewed in Detroit and he was asked about the possibility of bettering Howe's all-time scoring record, should Howe retire and Hull keep playing.

"First," Hull said, "I don't expect to be playing that much longer, but if I ever did reach that point where I tied Gordie's record, that's the day I would retire. I would never want to be the one who beat Gordie's record. He is the greatest."

When this was told to Howe, a frown crossed Gordie's face as he quietly replied, "Doesn't mean anything, because he won't ever come that close." Subject closed.

Jean Beliveau of the Montreal Canadiens, a former teammate of the Rocket, said, "Gordie Howe is the best hockey player I have ever seen!" The Rocket also has been quoted as acknowledging, "Howe is a better all-around player than I was."

With the record safely tucked away that night at the Olympia, Howe came out of the dressing room and confided to a friend, "Thank God that's over. It was getting so the boys wouldn't even have a beer with me."

That night, the mob of fans outside the dressing room door was much deeper than usual and Gordie stood for well over an hour signing autographs, accepting congratulations and with an emotionless expression returning his thanks. It appeared as if—and it actually was—that Gordie was truly embarrassed by the attention.

No matter that he might be tired, hungry, and thirsty, or that his wife was waiting with friends, Gordie stood and signed every autograph requested.

The next morning, the first man on the ice for practice? Yep, Gordie Howe, the famous No. 9, who was now number one in the N.H.L. record book.

Quite coincidentally, a dozen years later, Henry Aaron was saying just about the same thing after he became the home run king in Atlanta's Stadium. The pressure has to be terrible on an athlete who is on his way to what appears to be an obvious record-breaking feat. Everyone feels sure it will happen, but the pressure is on until it becomes a fact.

Gordie Howe is the greatest of them all,
   The greatest of them all, yes the greatest of them all.

Now, November 10, 1963, it was even more official.

12

Success, Pain, and Humor

With the start of the 1963-64 season, the experts had predicted at least a third place finish for the Detroit Red Wings in the National Hockey League. Perhaps the folks who cast such prophecies were especially enthusiastic because of the sure thing bet that Gordie Howe would become, early in the season, the world's greatest scorer in the history of professional hockey.

Of course, he did so, but it took several weeks to make that prediction an accomplished fact. Regardless, the Wings went skating their way through the defenses of their five opponents, sometimes quite ineptly, time and time again, and by the midway point of the season they had skidded to fifth.

When the experts debated the reasons for the Red Wings' skid during the first half of the 1963-64 season, the responsibility seemed to rest with Gordie Howe, who was temporarily off his usual game. Perhaps it was the pressure leading up to the record-tying and record-breaking goals, followed by a letdown after that period.

Whatever the reason, anytime that Gordie Howe's game is not up to its usual greatness, the team's own record is slipping. That's how important the big fellow, ole No. 9, was to the Wings in those halcyon days.

Regardless, Howe got back into the swing of things in the second half of the season and the Red Wings' team record improved. They finished fourth in the league, went to the playoffs and bowed in the finals.

Gordie's record for the season was 26 goals, 47 assists, and 73 total points—not his best season, by any means.

It did not still the debate, however, between the Howe fans and the believers in the retired and lamented Rocket Richard.

Dave Keon of the Toronto Maple Leafs was asked about the strength of the league one day and he opined, "There are four strong teams in the N.H.L., and two weak ones. The weak teams are Boston and New York. The strong ones are Toronto, Chicago, Montreal and Gordie Howe." This was in 1964, even with the Wings not at their best. The implication was very clear. Howe made the Red Wings go. Even during the first half of the season, when Howe scored only 15 goals, he was on the ice when most of the team goals were scored. The team scored 114 times in that first half, and 54 percent of them were scored while Howe was working. The Wings scored 54 percent of their goals during the 30 percent of the time when Howe was skating, and only 46 percent of their goals during the 70 percent of the time when he was resting. It seemed clear who motivated the team the most.

Maurice "Rocket" Richard, even though retired, was continually asked for his assessment of the fact that he no longer held the N.H.L. scoring record.

"Howe is a better all around player than I was, but I never thought he was too good a money player. I don't remember Howe scoring many game-winning goals. It always looked as though he would even be a greater player if he hustled more."

Even the Rocket was fooled by Howe's seemingly casual attack. League President Clarence Campbell answered those comments by producing records that showed that Howe, at that time, in 1964, held the league record for game-winning goals, 96, while the Rocket had only 83 game-winning markers to his credit.

Richard Beddoes, Stan Fischler, and Ira Gitler, three top hockey writers, all veterans and certainly no patsies for any player, described it this way in their 1971 book *Hockey!*—"As for Howe's image of nonhustling, it was merely a deception, partly a ploy, partly a link to his laconic background. He . . . has remained a small town westerner, drawling and taking his time about life.

"His laconic behavior on ice often lulls the opposition into thinking he's too tired to make a play or too disinterested. Howe, of course, measures his movements. A key to his longevity was his refusal to waste energy unnecessarily. When an opening developed, he'd move and often faster than anybody else on the ice. His skating style is what the pros call 'strong.' He has perfect balance and, as such, is difficult to upend. His strength is Promethean by hockey standards." (That means creative, boldly original.)

"He could carry the puck with one hand on the stick while warding off an opponent with the other. No other player in the N.H.L. but Howe is an ambidextrous shooter. And, while today's forward now relies so heavily on the slap shot, Howe remains a traditionalist, using a straight blade instead of a curved banana blade. His quick wrist shot has remained the most effective scoring weapon, per shot, in hockey."

The three expert writers continued: "The wrist shot is only a segment of the Howe arsenal. His strength is manifest in various ways. For years, he has outmuscled opponents and wrestled the puck from them in the corners from which goal-scoring passes are delivered. Or, he would camp in front of the net, seemingly impervious to the pushing and shoving of rival defensemen. In the 1965-66 season, Howe suffered through 13 games without a goal, but managed to break the slump by outpushing his rivals. His longtime teammate, Alex Delvecchio, remembered the episode. 'It was against the Rangers in New York. A shot—in fact I fired the puck—bounced off the seat of his pants past Jacques Plante into the Ranger net. That was muscle. The fact the puck went in off the seat of his pants is incidental. He was in the right place at the right time and he was shoving three guys out of the way. Each year he'll pick up nine or ten goals that way, just with strength, bulling his way through or past rival players.' "

Those are some of the opinions of three veteran hockey writers and a teammate, and such assessment obviously provokes the question: Does this man have no warts? Can he be for real?

A reporter out of Atlanta, Georgia, was spending much time in Detroit on business in 1963 and that was the time that "Gordie Howe, Greatest of Them All" was being worn out on the radio disc jockey shows, day after day, so he became quite aware of the greatness of Gordie Howe, at least in the hearts of Detroit people. A cynical reporter, a condition that seems to go with the territory, he wondered, what is Howe really like?

The reporter had a casual knowledge of hockey, from previous days in New England with the Providence Reds at the old Rhode Island Auditorium, then later in Washington, D.C., during World War II, when the Coast Guard fielded a professional hockey team in the American Hockey League with the Hershey Bears and other teams.

Being of an inquisitive nature, this fellow became a fascinated follower of the Red Wings and Gordie Howe. The first personal meeting came quite accidentally in the Detroit Metropolitan Airport, the pair introduced by Oakland Press hockey writer Jan Shaffer. Then there were more meetings, several of them, and the guy is still looking for the blemishes on the character of Gordie Howe.

Oh, there are a couple. He is a dirty, mean player, but as Alex Delvecchio said, "Dirty in a clean sort of way," and at times he may have a little ego problem, but who doesn't?

Gordie Howe may have inflicted physical damage on the enemy on the ice, but he has received more than his share in return, even in addition to the near-fatal injuries in 1950.

His face is smooth and angular, clearly defined, and it's virtually impossible to discern the location of the well over 300 surgical stitches that have gone into that pleasant face over the years.

"One year I had 50 stitches in my face," he recalled. "That was a bad year. Then I only got 10 stitches another year and that was a good year."

He has lost at least a dozen teeth during hockey skirmishes, two of them the first game he ever played with the Red Wings. He has undergone surgery for damaged knee cartilages, broken ribs, a broken wrist, several broken toes, a shoulder dislocation, many, many scalp wounds from other high stickers, and at least one painful ankle injury.

"It's not that bad," Gordie says, with a shrug. That's the nature of hockey, professional style. "One thing I learned early, from a very good team doctor, and that is a simple instruction, 'You can play over pain, but never play over an injury.' If you think you have an injury, like a cracked rib, for example, don't stay out there and take foolish chances. Get that injury taken care of right away. Pain, that's something else again. You can play in spite of something hurting, as long as it won't cause further damage."

Although he has been cut by pucks and sticks, the only visible scar on Howe's face is a small crescent on the left cheekbone. Then, of course, the constant eye blinking, the tic that was caused by the 1950 crash into the boards and the ensuing skull fracture and eye injury. That is the most noticeable, but then, that is Gordie Howe.

One long gash in his left thigh was so severe that the

doctor insisted on putting him under an anesthetic to clean the wound. In 1953 he played 15 games with his broken right wrist in a cast and he still led the league in both goals and assists, setting a scoring mark of 95 points. That's what he means by "playing over pain but not over an injury." The fracture was well taken care of and could not be worsened.

In 1958 his left shoulder was dislocated, and a week later he was hospitalized for ten days because of torn rib cartilages. His nose has been broken several times, and the skin over the bridge has been sewn so often it is said to be difficult to get a surgical needle through it.

In spite of all these injuries he missed only 42 games during his first 24 years in the N.H.L.

As has been said before, on the ice he is all business; off the ice and out in the public he is on the shy side. But in the locker room, after a game, he has a sense of humor that comes forth often, even though he is so frequently surrounded by inquisitive newsmen.

Gordie also has a habit of answering a question by making a question out of his answer. In one game there was an incident when he stopped a fast-skating opponent in mid-flight, virtually reaching out and lifting the enemy right off the ice, so there was daylight between the skates and the ice. Asked about it in the locker room, Howe quipped, "He must be slow. He sure stopped fast. Didn't you think he stopped fast?"

A sportswriter in his first year covering the Red Wings introduced himself to Howe in the locker room, "Hi, I'm Jan Shaffer of the *Pontiac Press.*" Howe bared his toothless grin as he stuck out his hand and said, "I'm Gordie Howe of the Detroit Red Wings," while the onlookers roared. "When everyone had stopped laughing," Shaffer said later, "I had forgotten the questions."

Later, the same writer approached Howe after a game, as Gordie was changing clothes and dressing. Gordie looked up at the writer, looked him right in the eyes and smilingly

Success, Pain, and Humor 91

answered his questions, never once pausing in the act of spraying foot powder all over Shaffer's shoes while a couple of teammates almost doubled up in laughter.

"There was another time," Jan continued, "when I was talking with Gary Unger after a game with Toronto when I felt a big hand hit me on the back, lifting me right off the floor. When I regained my balance, I looked around and there was Gordie staring at the ceiling as if he expected to see an elephant about to parachute.

" 'Is that the way you've gotten away with it all these years,' I asked Gordie. 'Naw,' he said grinning, 'Toronto holds a lot. Don't you think they hold a lot?' "

There was another game when Jim Rutherford, the Red Wing goalie, had posted a shutout, yet Howe had been voted the star of the game. On being asked about it later, he grinned and inquired, "Did my wife do the picking?"

Another sportswriter for the *Oakland Press,* in Pontiac, Michigan, got a surprise. Gordie reached out to shake hands and Jack O'Connell had a very unusual sensation. Howe still had his false teeth in the palm of his hand.

The young fans looking for autographs also see the Howe humor as well as the Howe patience. It has been traditional for fans to await the big guy after a game, lined up in the walkway from the locker rooms.

No matter how much he may be hurting, no matter how tired he may be, Howe will stand there until they are all taken care of. One young boy shoved his program forward and stuck his pen into Howe's hand and commanded, "Make it big!"

Gordie carefully drew a large black X on the program and handed it back. The boy looked, shook his head, and handed it right back to Howe, as the gathered crowd chuckled, so Gordie signed his regular autograph. The boy looked over the finished product and said, "I knew you could do better."

Five minutes later, Gordie noticed the same kid in the

crowd, staring curiously. "What's the matter now?" Howe asked. "Nothing, I'm just looking."

Then there was the 12-year-old who shoved a hockey stick at Gordie and demanded, "Sign it!" Howe looked at him a moment, and replied, "Say please." The kid came back with, "Okay, please." "Now," said No. 9, "put it all together."

"Sure. Gordie, will you please sign my damn stick?"

Gordie Howe, like the rest of us, learned a long time ago that you can't top the kids.

Even the adults seek the autographs, whether they spot him on the street or sitting in a restaurant. It happens all the time. While he is standing at the cashier's cage paying the check, they are already lining up in the path to the door, but they are usually apologetic. "Would you mind?"

When Gordie used to go home to visit his mother and father in Saskatchewan, he discovered that the easiest way was to quietly check into a motel with the folks, at least for the first couple of days. That was the only way they could get time alone to talk and get reacquainted.

Then there is this story Gordie told about his Dad: "Some guys came up to my father one day and asked him if he was the father of Gordie Howe and he answered, 'Yeah.' They offered him a drink and that was all for him that day. They must have put something in his drink and tried to roll him.

"That'll teach him," Gordie continued, still chuckling about the funny side of an unpleasant experience. "The next time anybody asks him if he's Gordie Howe's father, he'll say, 'No, never heard of the bum!'"

The price of fame—for athletes, and for relatives!

13

Red Wings Are Champions Again— For the Last Time!

At the close of the 1963-64 season, the Wings had acquired a new goalie. 21-year-old Roger Crozier was fresh out of a Black Hawk minor league team, having been obtained from Chicago in the trade of defenseman Howie Young.

Crozier played in fewer than a dozen games in that season, but enough so the Wings could see that the kid had a lot of promise. While the Wings did not plan it that way, Crozier became their regular goalie for the 1964-65 season. In order to protect the newcomer, Sid Abel exposed the veteran goalie Terry Sawchuk to the draft but figured he was safe because Terry was 34 years old. However, Abel was fooled when Toronto picked up Sawchuk.

Young Crozier was a little guy, only five feet, eight inches and barely 160 pounds, but he was fast on his skates and fast with his legs, hands, and body in blocking enemy goals. As one wag commented, being one of 14 children teaches a guy how to scramble.

Another thing happened for the Wings that year, 1964-65, and that was the return of veteran Ted Lindsay from a four-year layoff after leaving the Chicago Black Hawks in 1960. Lindsay wanted one more hurrah, this time playing for, instead of with, Sid Abel. Lindsay's 14 goals and 14 assists helped the Wings on their way to winning the N.H.L. championship, the last time that would happen for a long time, at least until another decade had passed.

Crozier recorded a fantastic 2.42 goals-against average for the season, which won him the Calder Trophy as the Rookie of the Year and earned him a spot on the next All-Star team, along with teammates Norm Ullman, Bill Gadsby, Alex Delvecchio, and the perennial Gordie Howe.

For the season, Ullman, Delvecchio, and Howe were the major scorers, Ullman hitting the cage for 42 goals, Alex getting 25 good ones, and Gordie scoring 29 with 47 assists. More and more Howe was passing to others for the glory shots.

The Detroit players went into the playoffs quite hopeful of making it all the way to the Stanley Cup, but Bobby Hull, coming off a bad late-season slump with the Chicago team, blasted eight goals in the seven-game series, the Black Hawks winning the playoffs and the right to meet Montreal for the Stanley Cup. Montreal downed Chicago in the seven-game series to end the season.

In the All-Star game, October 20, 1965, in the Montreal Forum, the 13,531 fans greeted Gordie Howe with a thunderous ovation as he was introduced at the start of the evening, and capped it with another standing ovation as he left the game in the final minute of play, all this in spite of the fact that his All-Stars had defeated their own Stanley Cup champs, the Canadiens, five to two.

In that game, Howe broke the old All-Star game record by scoring his eighth and ninth career goals and assisted with two others. The seven-goal record for All-Star games was held by none other than the Canadiens' great retired ace,

Red Wings Are Champions Again—For the Last Time?

Maurice Richard. Howe also increased his own All-Star career point total to 16, another new record. Howe also owned two more records for All-Star performance, as he was playing in his 17th game out of 19 seasons since he became an N.H.L. professional, and he was also the most penalized in All-Star competition, 21 minutes in those 17 years.

This was one of those classic games that make all sports so interesting when they come along. The All-Stars bounced back from a two-to-nothing deficit in the second period to forge ahead to a four-and-two lead right up to the last 90 seconds of play.

The All-Stars were playing short-handed because of a penalty against Harry Howell. Howe's final score, an unassisted beauty, was described by one player as Howe artistry at its best. Howe and Bobby Hull were killing the penalty as Howe intercepted the puck at his own blue line and streaked down the left side. Then, using Hull as a decoy, Gordie faked out Montreal defenseman Jacques Laperriere and rocketed the 30-foot shot like it was out of a cannon, past goalie Charlie Hodge. It was a perfect shot and the puck never left the ice.

Looking back two years, it was against those same two Montreal players that Gordie had scored his 545th goal to become the N.H.L. all-time leading scorer, defenseman Laperriere and goalie Hodge.

Montreal goalies Gump Worsley and Hodge had nothing to be embarrassed about that night, however, as between them they had made 25 saves. Ullman, Hull, Boston's John Bucyk, and Gordie Howe were too hot for them, that's all.

Chicago goalie Glenn Hall had to work the entire 60 minutes because Detroit's Roger Crozier was forced from the lineup because of illness, a heartbreaking situation for a rookie.

"I'm bushed," Hall lamented, then his eyes lighted up as he added, "The big devil has really slowed up, hasn't he? You know, they'll name this game after him, next. Did you ever see a prettier goal than his last one?"

Chicago coach Billy Reay, working his first All-Star game, added, "Gordie certainly played his game tonight, didn't he? Two goals and two assists, that's his game. I enjoyed the game from where I was standing," and then he started to dream a little, as he wrapped it up with, "Wouldn't it be nice to have that line—Ullman, Howe, and Hull—on one team all the time?"

Well, Reay had Hull on his team, but Ullman, Howe, and another incomparable, Alex Delvecchio, actually did make up the Red Wings' great new production line.

Gordie Howe had ended the 1964-65 season with 595 career goals, so in the fall of 1965 he was headed for another certain milestone, 600 goals, but this pressure was nowhere near as great as the start of that 1963-64 season. Actually, every time he shot a goal, regular season or All-Star game, he was creating a new record.

So, what's so important about 600 goals? The fans who like to quote record books feel it is important and so do the folks who keep the record books back in the N.H.L. headquarters.

The big thing about the 1965-66 season for Mr. Howe was that he was about to tie the 20-year longevity record held by Boston's Dit Clapper, who had retired the same year Howe was a Detroit rookie. Now, 19 seasons later, Howe was about to tie that record of playing for two uninterrupted decades—in fact, two decades in any order or disorder.

The average playing life in the N.H.L. was said to be 6.6 years. As any hockey enthusiast knows, Gordie Howe completed 25 years in the N.H.L. and two more in the W.H.A., but starting his 20th year, Howe never even dreamed that he would get that far. In fact, he often said he did not expect to complete 25 years.

Also, the present-day record books show that several

Red Wings Are Champions Again—For the Last Time?

players have since completed 21 years in the N.H.L. Harry Howell did 22 years in the N.H.L./W.H.A. and Howe's former Red Wings production linemate Alex Delvecchio did 22½ years and was still going strong when he was tapped, after 11 games into the 1973-74 season, to become the Red Wings coach, later the combination general manager and coach, and now general manager (1975-76).

But then, back in 1965, no one had the benefit of an accurate crystal ball, so going into his 20th season was a very big deal for Gordie Howe and friends.

He was asked if he thought he would go for 25 years and he quipped, "Well, the hours are good and the pay is excellent." Then, more seriously, he said, "I keep playing hockey because I like the game. Every game is a new challenge. Of course, every game is pain, too, but you learn to live with pain.

"I suppose I will play until the legs give out. I've seen it happen to others. The legs hurt so bad you can't go on. Sid Abel won the Most Valuable Player award and the next year his legs went. At the end of the season he told me his legs ached so bad he couldn't sleep at night and he was going to quit.

"Right now my legs hurt occasionally. I fool around in practice because what good is all this if you can't have some fun at it and then we have a hard practice and I'm tired. I have more bad games than I used to and I'm not as good as I was, but the statistics are holding up. When the time comes, I'm not so proud that I won't struggle through one more season, but I'll quit if I think I'm cheating the team or the fans."

Sid Abel, Red Wings coach, shuddered to think of the day that Gordie Howe would not be out there on the Olympia ice. "If his legs start to bother him," Sid explained, "we'll play him on defense, because that will be a little easier, but I'd hate to think of a Red Wings team without the big guy out there."

Regardless, the incomparable Gordie Howe was going into his 20th season with the N.H.L. and the Red Wings, and he was enthusiastic. Also, on that same team was defenseman Bill Gadsby, another close friend who was also starting his 20th year with the Wings and the league. Gadsby was a rookie the same year as Howe and they had seen a lot of good times and bad times together. There was one difference. Howe knew he was going to continue to play beyond that season. Gadsby was due to hang up the skates and the pads and the sticks. Two decades would be enough for Bill.

The new milestone, his 600th career goal, came on Saturday night, November 27, 1965, and once again was in the Montreal Forum. Five times Howe has scored a milestone marker against the Montreal Canadiens: the 100th goal was at Montreal in 1951, the 400th was at Montreal in 1958, the Richard-tying goal and new record goal came against Montreal at Olympia Stadium in October and November of 1963, and now this 600th shot was at Montreal.

Even though every goal he shoots is a new record, Gordie felt, after it was over, that there had been some pressure on him and the club. "I think the rest of the guys on the team are happy, too, because I think they were looking for me, trying to set me up."

Gary Bergman, a defenseman who had just been called up from the Wings' Memphis farm club in the Central Hockey League in time for the Montreal game, turned out to be the playmaker, exciting stuff for a rookie in his first game.

Bergman, Howe, and Don McKenney went down the ice together and Gary passed to McKenney, who shot wide of the Montreal goal, being tended by Gump Worsley. "The puck caromed around behind the net," Gary said later, "and I picked it up over in the corner to Worsley's right and passed it to Gordie and he flicked it right between Gump's pads."

Howe recalled, "I was skating backward across in front

of the net when Bergie tossed it to me. It went through Gump's pads kind of high in the corner. Gump fished the puck out of the net and handed it to me. He didn't say anything, just kind of gave me a look. After the game he got my autograph for his youngster."

It was the third time that Worsley had been the loser on a Howe milestone goal. The 500th had been scored against him when he was playing for the New York Rangers in 1962, and then there was the Rocket Richard-tying 544th at Olympia, October 27, 1963.

Gordie Howe, who seldom shows any emotion about accomplishments or honors, seemed to like this 600th marker. "You know there's a feeling of satisfaction to know that you've done something no one else has ever done," he told newsmen. "When you really stop to think about it, 600 goals is a heck of a lot of goals and it kind of scares you."

Howe had, no doubt, known to himself that time was creeping up on him, but this may have been the first time he indicated that thinking in public.

"You know, I'm going to make a will so these keepsakes can be distributed. My family comes first, of course, but I have a lot of valuable trophies, which are worth a lot of money, and I suppose some of these things belong in the Hall of Fame.

"Take the gold puck the Toronto Maple Leafs gave me for scoring 545, that's valuable. And the Canadiens gave me a valuable oil painting for the same goal. I have all these things in a room at home. I'll have to make some plans to see that it goes to the right places and, as I said, my family comes first."

Thinking back, it really was not too long ago that Gordie commented about milestone pucks and such objects by saying that "after a while they seem to lose their significance." Now, he was mellowing a bit, thinking along more sentimental lines.

He said the stick with which he scored number 600

would join the trophies along with the puck Gump had handed to him. "I'm having all the fellows autograph it so I'll have it as a keepsake."

Talking about any long-range plan, how many goals he might anticipate, he said, "I'm just taking them as they come, one at a time. However, the last goal I score, I made a promise to my wife on that one. She gets the puck."

Milestone goals, trophies, special awards, championships, they are all important in any man's career, but some of the most cherished moments have come to Gordie Howe not in competition.

"One of the greatest moments I ever had was not even involved in the game of hockey itself, but it did happen on the ice. The people of Detroit thought enough of me one night that they presented me with a 'night' of my own, a special 'Gordie Howe Night' at Olympia, that was along about 1960.

"They presented me with a new automobile, which was parked on the ice, covered with a huge sheet. They pulled the sheet off the car and there, sitting inside the car, were my Mom and my Dad."

Gordie wouldn't admit it as he recalled that very moving moment, but people who were there that night said the tears suddenly started streaming down the face of this usually unemotional man.

"Yes, that was one of the finest moments I ever experienced. My Mom had seen me play before, but my Dad never had. I'll never forget that night."

14

Welcome Home and Other Rewards

Gordie Howe stood in the center of a modern ice hockey arena in his home town of Saskatoon, Saskatchewan, Canada, and proclaimed, as he had in the past, "You know I am a man who shows very little emotion, but one of those days when I could not hide that emotion was right here in this rink in 1966, here in the city of Saskatoon. Down at the west end of the rink there was a platform, and Mom and Dad and the rest of the family sat up there and the people of Saskatoon were presenting Gordie Howe with a really, truly great day.

"I didn't say much or do much, but I felt emotionally inside and I feel the same way now. Here comes the old boy right now. My Dad's just coming into the building."

It was on July 22, 1966, that the 120,000 people of Saskatoon and the greats of the hockey world pulled out all the stops to pay homage to an all-time great hockey player.

To the sports world he is number one in hockey, but to these people in Western Canada he was Gordie Howe, the home town boy who comes back home every summer, back home to this big and dusty prairie city with its grain elevators marking its boundaries. This was the small town where Gordie Howe grew up from the time he was just nine days old, carried in his mother's arms as the family moved in from the farm country of nearby Floral where he was born.

This was the town where Gordie learned to skate almost as early as he learned to walk, and many of the people honoring him on this pleasant July Saturday were those with whom he went to school and men who worked with him on various construction jobs as he built up muscles, as well as those who knew him only from the image on their television screens as they watched the Detroit Red Wings play hockey.

Gordie Howe belonged to these people in Saskatoon and they were proud, although he had spent some 22 years working at his profession—playing hockey—in the United States, he always had remained a Canadian citizen, proud of his heritage.

Just as young Gordie and his friends used to skate for miles in the winter over this flat land, in summer you can see miles and miles of green and brown.

Saskatchewan Province was celebrating its own diamond anniversary in 1966 and the province had combined its resources and its officialdom with the City of Saskatoon to welcome home this native son and to name, in his honor, a new 350-acre sports complex, which included a football stadium, a baseball stadium, a golf course and, of course, a hockey rink.

Gordie and his family—wife Colleen and four children, Marty, Mark, Cathy, and Murray—had arrived late Friday night, and greeting them from every gaily decorated store window were huge pictures of Mr. Hockey, himself.

On Friday night, Mrs. Ab Howe had said, "I'm a little frightened by all this fuss. But one real nice thing is that all the children will be home together for the first time in 18 years."

Seventy thousand people lined the streets to salute the massive motorcade through the city, so gaily decorated with banners and flags and signs and pictures, the parade culminating at the new Gordie Howe sports complex, with a proclamation honoring the 38-year-old athlete read by Mayor E. J. Cole.

There on the platform at the west end of the hockey arena sat the family, headed by Mr. and Mrs. Ab Howe and their nine children and myriad grandchildren and other relatives. The five sisters all continued to live in Saskatoon— Edna, Vi, Gladys, Helen, and Joan. The three brothers were there: Vern, a career man in the Canadian Army at Kingston, Ontario; Norm, a career man in the Canadian Navy at Halifax, Nova Scotia; and Vic, who played three seasons with the New York Rangers, 1950-51; 1953-54; and 1954-55, and at this occasion a railway policeman at Moncton, New Brunswick.

Presented in Gordie's honor was a college scholarship to be awarded to Peewee hockey players. Tributes were read from Canadian Prime Minister Lester Pearson, Saskatchewan Premier W. Ross Thatcher, Saskatchewan Lieutenant-Governor R. L. Hanbidge, and, from south of the border, Michigan Governor George Romney.

Present to pay personal tribute were N.H.L. President Clarence Campbell, former Red Wings coach and general manager Jack Adams, the man who first "discovered" Gordie Howe at the Red Wings tryout camp in Windsor so long, yet not so long ago. Teammates Alex Delvecchio and Doug Barkley were there as well as representatives from most of the other teams in the N.H.L.

Ab Howe admitted he was still surprised that this gawky, clumsy son of his had turned out to be the greatest hockey player in the world, with 20 years behind him. "He was an awkward skater and was always hanging around in front of the net like Rocket Richard used to. First they made him a goalie, then they tried him on defense, but he was always down the other end anyway so they made him a forward. But I figured he might turn out pretty good because he always had a hockey stick in his hand. I think he used one for a lead pencil at school.

"I remember at one time he was a spectator at a commercial league game and a whale of a fight broke out on the ice. Gordie nipped down to one of the benches and grabbed a half dozen sticks while they were all fighting, and smuggled them out of the rink.

"He had a winter's supply of sticks from that. Maybe I should have belted him for it, but when a youngster is that determined it's a little rough."

The welcome home observance over, Gordie said so simply and honestly, "It's not a question of whether I'll ever forget this day and night here in Saskatoon. I'm worried I will never get over it."

Red Wings coach Sid Abel adopted a different kind of travel plan, which encouraged togetherness on the club, and Gordie told about that in a column he wrote for the *Detroit News* in 1966:

"Twenty seasons of traveling in the National Hockey League has been a weary round of one hotel room after another. And one hotel room is much the same as another. Some are large, and some are small and they all have telephones, radios and television sets, but there's a dreary sameness about them.

"With the Red Wings, however, there's something different each trip. That's your roommate. It's a practice the Wings started when Jack Adams was manager of the club and something that Sid Abel has resumed.

"On one trip, for instance, I may have Alex Delvecchio rooming with me in Toronto, then get Leo Boivin in Montreal and Bryan Watson in Boston. In New York I may have Roger Crozier. Sid and his assistant John Mitchell change the list for each trip and I think this is good.

"Back when I first joined the club the only roommate I had for years was Ted Lindsay. When you room with a player you have a tendency to go around with him all the time, and in my case for years the only player I really knew well on the club was Ted. This may sound strange because I have played with hundreds of players.

"I don't know how the other clubs in the N.H.L. operate, but I think our system is a good one. You get to know everybody on the club and there is less chance of cliques forming. You get a real team spirit.

"There's always talk of course that players like to room alone. This is nonsense. I remember once last winter when Watson wound up without a roommate. He complained all the next day that he couldn't sleep because he hadn't anyone to talk to. But, as everyone probably knows, Bryan is a compulsive talker.

"Over the years with different roommates, I think my strangest experience was with Cummy Burton. He asked me to lock all the doors and windows and then told me that he walked in his sleep. Fortunately, he didn't while he was with me, but I understand he did a few times while he was rooming with some of the other fellows."

Howe mentioned that he had played with hundreds of teammates. Actually 209 Red Wings teammates in those two decades.

A knee injury suffered in an exhibition game forced Howe into a slow start, so the Wings were in a slump early in the 1966-67 season. Strange as it may seem, Gordie was the man who motivated the team, and if he was down, so were the Wings.

As the knee condition improved, so did his skating and so did his play-making. Gordie wouldn't use the bad knee as an excuse, but he did admit it wasn't as good at the start of the season: "There's no point in denying that."

Sid Abel pointed out, "Gordie is skating as well as he has in the last three or four years. Certainly it took him a while to get over the knee injury, but you have to remember he is 38. That's not old by any means, but he just can't bounce back as fast as a youngster. With him going again I figure the whole club will perk up."

Ross "Lefty" Wilson, the Red Wings trainer for eight years, was commenting, "Gordie hates tape. Until he banged up his knee I hadn't been near him with a roll of tape for I don't know how many years. You just go years without doing anything for him. If every hockey player were like him, I'd be out of a job, but there's only one Howe."

Veteran Alex Delvecchio, playing with Howe for 16 years, offered his assessment: "Slowed down? Not so you'd notice it. Sure it has taken him a little longer to get going this season, but he's finally in top shape. Watch him. He's fooling around with the puck again. When he does that he's not worried about his knee, his wind or going against the best in the league."

Ted Hampson had joined Howe and Delveccio on the most recent version of the famed production line, and he said, "There's only one problem playing on a line with Gordie and Alex. You find yourself standing around watching them. I sometimes feel like I'm a spectator. It's like a wonderful dream, a wonderful dream come true playing with them.

"Everybody talks about goals, games, seasons in the league, awards, anything and everything when it comes to Howe, but there's so much that goes unnoticed. Watch him in the corners, pushing defensemen around, hounding the forwards. He contributes so much that never shows up in the statistics."

"What more can you say? He's the greatest on ice, but that's not what I'm talking about," contributed Bryan Watson. "The greatest part of Gordie is found off the ice—

the way he treats a rookie, his concern about every guy on the team, his family. Maybe it's his understanding, his way of accepting every guy for what he is. You don't have to be in the hall of fame to have Gordie on your side."

For years it was little known to the public, but well known among the players, that practically every newcomer to the team was soon invited to dinner with the Howe family, nothing formal or pretentious, they were just treated like family. That was Gordie's and Colleen's way of breaking the ice for the rookies, because Gordie remembered so vividly his early lonesome days in Galt, Omaha, and Detroit.

A new honor was to come his way in February of 1967. The New York Rangers had unveiled a new award the previous year, in honor of their long-time general manager and coach the late Lester Patrick, the award to be presented for outstanding service to hockey in the United States, the recipient to be chosen by a six-man committee consisting of the President of the N.H.L., an N.H.L. governor, a hockey writer for a U.S. national news service, a nationally syndicated columnist, a former player who is in the Hockey Hall of Fame, and a sports director of a U.S. national radio and television network. All but the N.H.L. President to be rotated annually.

The first winner, early in 1966, had been Jack Adams, the former veteran coach and general manager of the Detroit Red Wings, and at this time president of the Central Hockey League.

Gordie Howe had been the unanimous choice of the panel to be the second recipient. When Howe was notified about the award, he was asked to select the greatest stars he had played with and against, and those he had chosen were seated at the head table for the presentation.

Howe's selection of opponents: Maurice "Rocket" Richard, Doug Harvey, and Bill Durham of the Montreal Canadiens; Milt Schmidt and Fernie Flaman of the Boston Bruins; and Doug Bentley of the Chicago Black Hawks.

Former teammates honored by Howe were Sid Abel, Ted Lindsay, Bill Gadsby, defenseman Bob Goldham, and Harry "Apple Cheeks" Lumley, a goalie.

As the presentation of the large trophy was being made by Lynn and Muzz Patrick, sons of the late Lester Patrick, Gordie proved he was just as quick in a banquet hall as on the ice. The trophy was fumbled by the presenters and headed for the floor, but Gordie's split-second reflex reaction snatched it in midair.

Jack Adams, the first winner, told the crowd, as well as Howe, "Gordie, I'm happy and proud that this trophy has been awarded to you. If it hadn't been for you, I wouldn't have won the first one."

It was recalled that a year before, at the first trophy dinner, Gordie had told Jack Adams, "Close to my father, up very close, it's you."

Ted Lindsay, who had played with Gordie on the original great production line of the Wings, said, "Gordie carried me for years on left wing and you are looking at the last of the great dedicated athletes." Gordie was to remember those words several years later, with sadness.

Recalling that this award was created by the New York Rangers, and that Gordie had first tried out for the Rangers and had rejected their contract offer, Gordie explained, "I was homesick and I'm glad I wound up with Detroit. It just shows how loneliness pays off."

After winning the league championship in 1964-65, but losing in the playoffs, the Wings started to skid. For 1965-66 they finished fourth in the league, good enough to get in the playoffs, but they were defeated in six games by the Montreal Canadiens. They finished fifth, out of the playoffs, in 1966-67 and the next season, 1967-68, found them sixth, out of the playoffs for the second straight year, only the fourth time in 20 years.

Gordie Howe had been holding his own, however, with 29 goals and 46 assists in 1965-66, followed by 25 goals and

Welcome Home and Other Rewards

40 assists, and now, as he reached his 40th birthday, 39 goals and 43 assists, for 82 points, his best total in five years.

This would be the 12th time in a 22-year career span that Howe had scored more than 30 goals.

With his Wings in a slump, Howe's son Mark was playing on an unbeaten junior team. "I told him he should win," Gordie said, "because he was playing against a bunch of kids." Mark's answer was, "What about you?"

As Gordie approached his 40th birthday in March of 1968, the *New York Times* said: "The shoulders seem to slope a trifle more. Perhaps it also takes him a bit longer to change from his Detroit Red Wings uniform into street clothes after a game . . . [yet] . . . Gordie Howe at 39 is capping the kind of a season that men 15 years his junior envy. . . . A week ago he scored three goals in a single game, the 16th time he had accomplished the feat.

"Does that mean he's better than ever? 'Maybe not better,' says Alex Delvecchio, his long-time center, 'but just as good. And, that's pretty good.' "

The *Times* continued: "In a game where players dash up and down the ice at speeds up to 30 miles an hour, Gordie Howe ranks as something of a medical marvel. Howe has no trouble keeping up with the younger members around the league, although even his coach and long-time linemate Sid Abel admits that some nights are tougher than others for Gordie.

" 'He has his flat games just like everyone else,' Abel told the Associated Press, 'but he's still the greatest.' "

The *Times* continued: "Gordie Howe on a bad night is head and shoulders above most players on an average night. Does Howe feel 40? 'Forty? Well that's not very old, you know. I feel fine, thank you.' "

Even Gordie Howe could not imagine the years that were still to come, the hockey playing productive years, more new records being established every game.

15

A Couple of Milestones and Surgery

It was with mixed emotions that Gordie Howe took aim at the 1968-69 season, his 23rd. It has been said that life begins at 40, but Mr. Hockey, the still able No. 9, wasn't quite positive of that. Two seasons before, the Red Wings had finished way down in fifth place in a six-team league, completely out of the playoffs.

Then with the expansion of the N.H.L.—doubling in size to 12 teams—for the 1967-68 season, Howe had realized a good year personally with 39 goals and 43 assists, but his team had finished in the basement of the new Eastern Division, sixth in a six-team group.

However, the Wings had added a new man, Frank "Big M" Mahovlich from the Toronto Maple Leafs, and the newest production line of Howe, Mahovlich, and Delvecchio was working well. On top of that, the team had a new coach, former teammate Bill Gadsby, with Sid Abel now concentrating on being general manager, rather than trying to handle both jobs.

Howe had never pressed for more money in all the years he had been with the Wings. He was usually the first to sign every year and is generally believed to have accepted whatever he was offered, in sharp contrast with the sports world of the 70s, with agents and strikes and hassles.

The only time Howe came close to hassling over the deal was the first day he signed with Jack Adams, signing the deal with which he went first to the amateur Galt Red Wings, then to the minor league team at Omaha.

That first day, after he had signed, coach and manager Jack Adams found him outside the office, looking unhappy. Gordie explained, "You promised me a Red Wings jacket and I still don't have it." He got the jacket, of course, and if he had asked for more money along the line he probably would have received that, too, but this was not Gordie Howe's style.

The Detroit sportswriters and broadcasters had been getting on the Red Wings club management, Sid Abel and owner Bruce Norris, about the lack of big money for their players, commensurate with the times.

Regardless of the reasoning, in the fall of 1968, Bruce Norris and Sid Abel tore up Gordie's existing two-year contract and wrote a fresh one for two years, rumored to be about $75,000 a year, a figure that Howe, years later, confirmed.

Gordie figured that he had now played in 1,472 N.H.L. hockey games; the league was now operating with a 74-game season because of the expansion and that would end at 1,620 games when his contract expired in two years, at age 42 with 24 seasons behind him.

He had scored 688 regular-season goals, going into these two supposedly final years, so he would probably wrap it up with a lifetime total of 750.

Yes, this two-year contract would probably do it for Gordie Howe, the first time he had ever publicly even considered retirement. Nothing definite, you understand, just a little casual thinking about the future. He still reserved the

A Couple of Milestones and Surgery

right to play as long as he could get the job done.

However, he did have to admit that the fun was going out of the game, with his team skidding out of playoff contention two seasons in a row, even though he had finished the last season the third best scorer in the league. Only Stan Mikita of Chicago, with 87 points, and Boston's Phil Esposito, with 84, had topped Gordie's 82.

Abel told newsmen that he had talked with Gordie about rewriting the contract "just about the time the season opened, but because of the size of the figure involved, Gordie sat down with Mr. Norris and they came up with the salary figure. Gordie's real happy about it and so are we."

It was also announced that Howe had been named a vice-president of the Norris-owned Detroit-based insurance company, Olympia Agencies, Inc. More on that later.

"I can honestly admit the game is getting tougher," Howe said. Coach Gadsby added, "After all the guy is only human. But what a human!" Gadsby looked off into space for a moment, then said, thoughtfully, "It will be a sad day around here when he does hang them up. Frankly, it certainly will be a big difference to look down that bench and not see the big No. 9 there. There's no denying it, with Gordie gone, it will be a sad day here."

The next milestone goal was not long in coming—No. 700. Howe had finished the previous season with a total of 688 goals in regular seasons. He had topped over 700 in regular season plus playoffs, but the big one in the books is for regular seasons only.

It came on December 4, 1968, before a thin Wednesday night attendance of only 4,414 paid in Pittsburgh's Civic Arena. The Penguins had scored first.

Gordie had borrowed a hockey stick from teammate Bruce MacGregor because he was unhappy with "the last batch they sent me. They were horrible. The shaft of Brucie's stick is not as flexible, although I would still like a stick with a stiffer shaft."

Regardless of the flexing of the shaft, they were only

seven minutes into the first period, behind one to zip, when Frank Mahovlich took the puck away from the Penguins' Charlie Burns behind the Pittsburgh net and passed it to Alex Delvecchio along the boards. Alex zapped the puck to Gordie, who was just 20 feet out from the net, to goalie Les Binkley's right.

Gordie whipped the puck along the ice into the far corner of the net. "I didn't even look when I took the pass from Frank," he said. "I just snapped it along the ice."

Referee Ron Wicks took the puck from the net and handed it to Gordie and most of the fans stood and cheered. That was it and play resumed immediately. As Howe once said, these things lose their significance after a while. Detroit won the game seven to two.

"I'm glad it's over," Gordie said after the game. "I must feel 10 pounds lighter."

The next milestone was a strange one, happening before a sellout crowd of some 15,000 fans at hometown Olympia, as the Red Wings took on the Chicago Black Hawks. That night, Howe was bothered by an upset stomach, his bruised ribs ached, his legs were logy, but he told Coach Gadsby, "I'll try, but don't expect too much."

Gordie's first goal of this evening came when he stickhandled around a Chicago defender, feinted the goalie out of position, and fired the puck into the net. That was goal number 714. Later he took a pass, down the ice he went, and fired again for number 715, and the crowd stood and roared.

What was the significance of number 715? One more than Babe Ruth's home run record. "We had to reach into another sport to find any comparable achievement," one man explained. "For in hockey, Gordie Howe is beyond comparison."

One more than Babe Ruth's total home run production. Long before Hank Aaron officially bettered the Babe's home run record, Gordie Howe was well on his way to goal number 800. No way that baseball will catch up, at least in the foreseeable future.

A Couple of Milestones and Surgery

The Red Wings improved a little in 1967-68, moving up to a fifth-place finish in the Eastern Division, but still out of the playoffs for the third straight year, a disastrous record. For Howe, it was an entirely different year, the best he ever had. He had scored 44 goals, the fifth time he had topped the 40 mark; he was credited with 59 assists, the best ever. His previous high had been 49 assists, in 1960-61. And he had a total of 103 points, again the best ever, the first time he had topped 100.

Admittedly this was in a high-scoring year, probably because of a longer season by six games and against some expansion teams. Howe was the third highest point getter in the N.H.L. that season, being topped by Boston's Phil Esposito and Chicago's Bobby Hull.

Detroit News sportswriter Bill Brennan had become an especially keen observer of Mr. Gordon Howe, hockey player, as the years began to add up. As Gordie was winding down his 23rd season in the N.H.L. (his best ever), and as Gordie approached his 41st birthday, Bill Brennan asked a long string of questions and Gordie's answers included a couple of surprises as well as some interesting introspection. Here is the report:

Is the pressure tough to live with?

Not really. They [the management] expect you to eat, sleep and live hockey. To me that's a good way to go crazy. I don't believe in it. For one thing you have to take care of your body. That is the hockey player's equipment. You keep in shape and you watch your weight. You eat the things you know you should. Take the day of the game. I would love a steak, but I have eggs instead. Why? Because I feel stuffy if I have a steak. I feel I play better with eggs."

You will be 41, completing 23 years. How many more?

"I plan to try for 25, that is if I stay healthy. I have another year on my contract which takes me to the end of next season [the 24th]. Then I may try for one more. I've been thinking about it for a while. I look on it this way. I've always said that if I had two bad years in a row I'd quit.

Well, this one has been good, so even if I have a bad one next year, it would still give me the following season to prove myself. Twenty-five—a quarter of a century. It really sounds something when you say it like that, eh? But 25 is a nice round figure."

After that, coaching maybe?

"I don't think so. I don't want to sound like I'm crying, but I've been in hockey a long time. Coaching I think is tougher than playing. My family is growing up and I've missed it. In the summer I'm away on the tour for the department store chain I work for [Eaton's in Canada]. I don't see my family for a month and the children all look as though they've grown a foot. They go skiing and then come home and I hear them talk about it. I'm not part of it. I'm missing this part of their lives. No, I think when I quit as a player I will just take it easy."

You mentioned this was a good season, 40 goals and more assists than ever before. Do you have an objective?

"Sure, to get into the playoffs [which they did not]. When the season started, my objective was to score 30 goals. I knew I'd be playing with Frank Mahovlich and Alex Delvecchio and I figured with those two my chances would be pretty good to hit 30. I'm over that now, so I have to be happy.

"We were talking about pressure a little while ago. There is pressure in this way in playing with Frank and Alex. It means that we have to do the scoring. That's the way things have been this year. We have to stir things up. We don't manage to do it all the time, but we do have to try. I suppose there is pressure when you look on it that way."

You have played with two famous left wingers. First, Ted Lindsay, a charter member of the "Production Line" with yourself and Sid Abel. Now there is Frank Mahovlich since a year ago when Toronto traded him to Detroit. How do they compare?

"Well they are different, eh? Like night and day. In fact

A Couple of Milestones and Surgery

I can't figure two guys being any more different. Ted was rambunctious. He'd lay the lumber on everybody. Frank skates for those holes. I've never seen a player who could skate for those holes better, although Ted was pretty good at it.

"There is a difference between being quick and fast. Ted was quick. He was like a quarter horse. Say take from the net to the blue line, he could beat Frank. But from the net to the far blue line, Frank could beat Ted. Frank is fast.

"Strength—you have a difference there, too. Ted had stamina, but Frank has strength. Frank rushes down the ice a couple of times and then he must head for the bench to get some wind. Ted could do it maybe four, five or six times before he needed to collect wind. That's what I mean by stamina and strength. Frank is real strong. He can skate right over people, but he doesn't have the stamina, for a big guy, that Ted had. Maybe that is the reason. He is so much bigger than Ted.

"Frank is not tough to play with, but you have to lead him pretty good with a pass. Maybe more than the average guy. Ted could take a pass on his skates or behind him or wherever it happened to be. Frank is a positional player. Ted wasn't. He was a darter. He'd dart all over. Frank is easier to play with in that way because you know where he'll be. He goes up and down. With Lindsay and myself, when we were together we roamed all over."

And Delvecchio?

"Now you are talking about the key man on the line. Everybody must do his share, but being the center, Alex is the guy that makes things tick. He's a great center, eh?"

Do you have some other feelings about the game after all these years?

"Well, pep talks don't win hockey games, especially with older players. You start getting up for the game the day of the game. I still get nervous. I suppose I always will. But that disappears once the game starts. Then when the game is over you try to put it out of your mind. You don't take it home with you."

How about the schedule where you play three games in four nights? You say 40 "is a ripe age for a hockey player." Does it bother you?

"I've found that the older I get the more rest I need. It has become increasingly important. I need more sleep. This is something that you must make provision for. You must schedule your day and even things like shopping must be put aside for another time."

Isn't the third game of three-in-four tougher?

"Frankly, this puzzles me. I've found that quite often I'm better in the third game than in the first two. We had that situation recently and I felt tired before the game started and told them, 'Don't count on me for much tonight.' So what happens, I get a hat trick. I put it this way, it doesn't seem to affect me. However, after that third game I'm really beat. But it's an honest fatigue. The body is drained."

The two seasons prior to this one, the Red Wings missed the playoffs. The defense got a lot of the blame. Did they deserve it? (Note: two weeks after this response, the Wings missed the playoff for the third year in a row.)

"Well, we have a much better defense this season. Bob Baun has been a standout for us since the first game. Poul Popiel has developed and so has Ron Harris. And while I'm at it take Popiel. There is a young guy who is anxious to buy a home in Detroit. He says he feels that he is welcome, that he's wanted. He said the other clubs were nice to him, but the Wings really made him feel like he was wanted. That's good, eh?" (Note: Poul Popiel was drafted away from Detroit by Vancouver, then he went to the W.H.A. and was playing with the Houston Aeros when Gordie got there, teammates again.)

Has Coach Bill Gadsby, an ex-defenseman, made the difference with the defense?

"I think probably. It only takes a few do's and don'ts to

MR. HOCKEY

A seventeen-year-old Gordie Howe in 1945, playing with the Omaha farm club team.

Right: Gordie Howe, a Red Wing rookie, eighteen years old, 1946.

Below: The famed Detroit Red Wings "production line" of (l to r) Gordie Howe, Sid Abel, and Ted Lindsay.

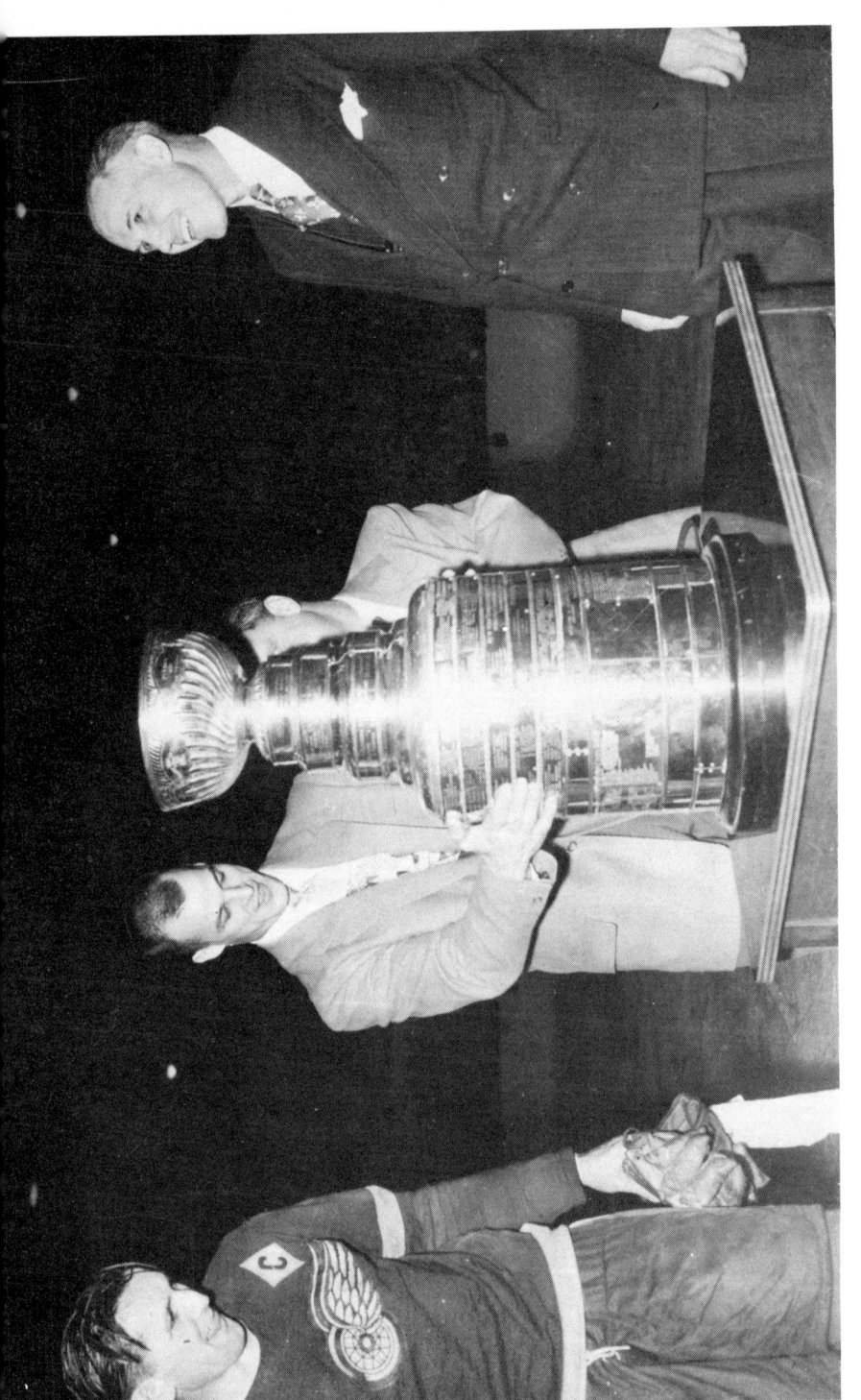
The Stanley Cup, won by the Detroit Red Wings in the spring of 1952, with Sid Abel, left, team captain; Jack Adams, coach; Jim Norris, owner; and N.H.L. President Clarence

November 5, 1953: Gordie Howe (in white) scores his 215th goal for the Red Wings against the New York Rangers at Olympia. (Not a milestone, just good action.)

In this 1960 photo, Gordie Howe scores for the Red Wings, rifling the puck past sprawled goalie John Bower of the Toronto Maple Leafs. Larry Hillman makes a last-moment move to try to prevent the goal.

Gordie Howe scores his 500th goal against New York Rangers goalie Gump Worsley, March 14, 1962. The Rangers player behind Howe is Doug Harvey, now the assistant coach and chief scout for the Houston Aeros, the man who first recommended that the Aeros draft Mark and Marty Howe.

October 27, 1963: Gordie Howe scores goal number 544 for the Detroit Red Wings, tying the record established by Maurice "Rocket" Richard. Sprawled in front of the Montreal Canadien goal is goalie

help a guy, you know, and Bill talks pretty good to them. All coaches get mad and chew players out. Bill is no different than the rest. He's a good coach. I like his practices better than Sid's. He mixes things up. They are more interesting. There is nothing more deadly than doing the same things over and over again day after day. We have some real good practices with Bill."

How come the Wings have problems [playing against] expansion teams?

"I can give you a good reason for last year. Baz Bastien [pro scouting director] was giving us a talk at a team meeting about one of the expansion clubs. Say St. Louis. He listed Glenn Hall and a few other veterans and then he said, 'They have five American Leaguers and five Central Leaguers.' I counted our players in the room and what do you think? We had one more minor leaguer than they had. That to me is expansion hockey.

"Now we've a better club. That big deal with Toronto didn't hurt. Especially with guys like Pete Stemkowski and Gary Unger [coming to the Wings]. And getting Wayne Connelly from Minnesota for Danny Lawson didn't hurt, either. Hey, while we are at it, that guy in Chicago [Manager Tommy Ivan], he must have nightmares when he thinks of that Phil Esposito trade [from Chicago to Boston, where he now leads the league in scoring]."

("That man in Chicago" Tommy Ivan, who had once been Gordie's coach with the Wings, redeemed himself the following year, 1969-70, for letting Phil Esposito get away, by drafting younger brother Tony Esposito, a goalie. Young Tony won the Calder trophy as Rookie of the Year, plus the Vezina trophy, which goes to the team that allowed the fewest goals, while big brother Phil was second in the league in scoring.)

In Detroit, the Red Wings bounced back from a three-year toboggan slide and finished third in the league's Eastern Division, candidates to take the playoffs and go into the

Stanley Cup fray. Candidates, that is, until the Chicago Black Hawks beat them in four games.

For Gordie Howe, finishing the second year of his $75,000 contract, it was not a bad year at all. He played in every game again, scored 31 goals, his 14th season with more than 30. He had 40 assists for 71 points, the 18th year he had topped 70.

The grand total now stood at 1,624 games played in 24 seasons, 763 goals scored, 994 assists and 1,757 points, all N.H.L. records. His closest pursuers were Bobby Hull on goals and teammate Alex Delvecchio in the assists and points departments.

Before leaving on the long bus ride to Chicago for the playoffs, Gordie paused long enough at Olympia on March 31, 1970, to be presented with a huge birthday cake, labeled for No. 9 on his 42nd. It was pointed out that Gordie had said he would quit if he had two bad seasons in a row, and this wasn't one of them, so the speculation was that he'd be around for numbers 25 and 26, maybe. Gordie wasn't talking.

Howe did not make a big thing of it, but it was no secret that he had been playing every game in pain because of the arthritis in both wrists, the left one the more painful.

Without any advance notice, Gordie slipped into the University of Michigan Medical Center just before Memorial Day for what turned out to be a two-hour operation on his left wrist. Dr. Robert Bailey, the orthopedic surgeon, explained that Gordie had "traumatic arthritis of the radio-navicular joint of the left wrist" and that "we removed loose fragments of bone and also took out the dead navicular bone."

The left arm remained in a plastic cast for six weeks and physical therapy was used to strengthen the wrist. It is a fact that Gordie Howe has been a great fan of Dr. Bailey for a span of time, and still is. Whatever Dr. Robert Bailey says about Gordie's arthritis is gospel.

A Couple of Milestones and Surgery

Before the summer ended, Gordie was back shooting golf in the 70s and low 80s, but the wrist continued to bother him, and Dr. Bailey said it would until the bones settled in the hand.

16

Another Two-Year Contract, and 100 Grand

With the surgery on his left wrist an accomplished fact, it became apparent that Gordie Howe would continue past that 24th season just completed, so there was much speculation about the direction the new contract would take.

As Gordie recalled, "The press media here in Detroit kept insisting in the papers and on the radio and television that I should be the first hundred thousand dollar a year hockey player in the N.H.L. so when I went in to negotiate the contract, the $100,000 was there."

Howe signed for two more years at a hundred grand each. "I never had an ambition to be a fat millionaire," Gordie said, "just comfortable with some extras.

"I'll be 44 in two years and I'm pressing my luck now. The new contract is real handsome because it's my last and it's not so much for these two years coming, but for the dedication of the last 24."

Howe continued to deny that he gets away with more

infractions than others. "I remember George Gravel, the little French-Canadian referee, used to get me and he'd say, 'Ho-ho, I caught you dat time!' I liked him. I like it when the referees and linesmen have a little humor. Gravel would keep up the chatter and if I was slow coming out of the game, he'd yell, 'Hurry! Hurry! You're caught!' I'd just tell him not to make me laugh because it would look bad if I was laughing and going to the penalty box."

Then, as if this was explanation enough about the penalties, "It's a man's game."

With the additional income from the previous two seasons at $75,000 each, and the promise of $100,000 a year, the Howes became involved as investors in the cattle business with a friend, on a cattle ranch at Grass Lake, about 50 miles west of Detroit. Also, there was the vice-presidency in Bruce Norris' insurance agency and he was getting the feel of that business as quickly as possible.

For the start of the 1970-71 season, Red Wings owner Bruce Norris made a strange move, at least it turned out that way as far as the press, the players, and especially the fans were concerned.

Norris hired as the new coach a fellow named Ned Harkness, who had no previous pro hockey experience. He had been the lacrosse coach at Cornell University.

Immediately Harkness invoked new rules and adopted what the players called a "rah-rah" system right out of the college sports textbooks. The orders, which they felt were petty and more suited to schoolboys than to grown professionals, went over like a lead balloon.

Veteran defenseman Carl Brewer walked out on the team even before the season started, and sat out most of the year, rather than submit. He was subsequently traded to St. Louis.

Harkness made many trades and tried to negotiate other deals, most of which were unpopular in Detroit, such as Pete Stemkowski to the New York Rangers in November of 1970,

Another Two-Year Contract, and 100 Grand

then Gordie's stalwart left-wing partner, Frank Mahovlich, to the Montreal Canadiens in January, 1971, followed by center Bruce MacGregor and defenseman Larry Brown to the New York Rangers in February.

In 1970-71, the first year of the unpopular Ned Harkness era, the Wings skidded to seventh place in the Eastern Division, winning only 22 games, losing 45, and tying 11, once again out of the playoffs—in fact, starting a new string of at least five years in which they missed the playoffs.

Through it all, Gordie Howe and Alex Delvecchio continued to try and do their best, to put up a good front, to keep out of the hassles in the locker room and the front office, but neither would they lie to the press or fans when cornered.

How they kept their cool, along with other great Wings players, will always be a mystery. It seemed that when a player spoke up, spoke his mind, he was immediately on the possible trade list as management tried to purge the team of those they felt were trouble-makers.

If Harkness ever considered trading Gordie Howe, and there is no evidence that he did, it would not have worked. The Detroit sports fans would have gone back to the way it was done in the old days and run him out of town on the proverbial rail.

This was not to be a good season for Gordie Howe, any more than it was for the Wings, as he would wrap it up with 23 goals, 29 assists, and 52 points, after playing in only 63 games. Even the time in the penalty box that year was to reach a new low, only 38 minutes. When Gordie Howe is no more aggressive than that, things have to be bad!

Through it all, Gordie still indicated that he would play the following season, his 26th in the N.H.L.

Whether someone sensed that Gordie would hang it up, or whatever the reason, they tossed a 25th anniversary ceremony for Howe on the closing home night of the season at Olympia Saturday night, April 3, 1971, between the periods of the Chicago Black Hawks game.

Every fan attending received a commemorative badge reading: "Silver Anniversary, Gordie Howe" and there was the traditional cake, the gifts, the greetings from public officials, and a tremendous ovation from the fans and the assembled Red Wings and Black Hawks.

Three nights earlier, Wednesday, March 31, Gordie had observed his 43rd birthday on the ice, with the Toronto Maple Leafs presenting him with a silver tray.

The season ended Monday night on the road against the New York Rangers, the team that had originally invited him to the tryout camp and had offered to sign him way back in the summer of 1943.

After some rest and relaxation, Gordie became more involved in the cattle ranch investment and in the Norris-owned insurance business. In mid-May, 1971, he still had not made up his mind whether to play one more year, at $100,000, or to hang up the skates.

"As long as my hand continues to feel good, I'll be back," he said then. "It's been feeling pretty good since the season ended and all I can say now is that I'll be playing when we open camp."

Howe had discussed the situation with Bruce Norris, who said that Gordie could continue to play hockey and at the same time work into the insurance business. Howe was also made a vice president of Norris' new holding company, Norin Co., organized to consolidate Bruce's many enterprises other than the Red Wings.

Ten insurance agencies around the country had been brought together under the Norin Co. banner, along with property holdings and a Homosassa Springs 43,000-acre recreational and other use development in Florida, near Tampa.

"Even if I don't play next year," Gordie added, "I'll stay with the hockey club and work as an assistant" to new coach and former teammate Doug Barkley.

Harkness's failure as a professional hockey coach had become quite apparent, so he was moved up to general manager, with Barkley signed as coach.

17

Time for the Decision

Gordie Howe, his wife Colleen, and the four Howe children tried to relax a bit in the summer of 1971, after Gordie had completed his 25th year with the Red Wings, 27 years in organized hockey, but it wasn't all that easy.

Things were going great for the two older sons, Marty and Mark, who had helped lead the Junior Red Wings to the championship in the Southern Ontario Junior Hockey League, the first American junior hockey club ever to play in a Canadian league.

Colleen Howe was very active in the Junior Red Wings; many said that she was the spark plug, the one who made the whole thing go. She raised funds, she sold tickets, she drove hundreds of miles during the winter, and she had a heck of a time trying to maintain a personal attendance schedule at the Junior Wings games and the N.H.L. Red Wings home games.

Both Marty, then 17 years old, and Mark, then 15, close

to 16, had been elected to the S.O.J.H.L. All-Star team, and young Mark won the Most Valuable Player award, as well as the trophy for the outstanding forward. Marty was being rated an excellent defenseman.

They had purchased a nice little summer place on Bear Lake near Kalkaska, about in the center of the state, a couple of hundred miles north of Detroit. The cottage, with lots of bedrooms and a large family room, dinette, and kitchen, was surrounded by huge trees, with friendly neighbors on both sides, several families who had been friends even before they all moved there. Sailboats, motorcycles, automobiles—anything you could want for recreation were in abundance.

There is a long set of steps from the porch, which spreads across the front of the house facing the lake. Gordie kept in shape running up and down those steps—83 of them—several times a day when they went swimming or boating.

In addition, he was learning the insurance business, a crash course to go with the new vice-presidency, and then the endless questions whenever he was out in the public—"Will you play another year? Will you retire?"

Quite honestly, he didn't know. He knew there was little chance of fulfilling that long-cherished dream to play with his two older sons on the Howe line for the Red Wings.

That had been a pleasant experience when the Red Wings had played the Junior Wings for the benefit of the March of Dimes a season or so back. Gordie had switched sides for the night and had skated with the Juniors, the three forming the Howe line, which thrilled the more than 14,000 fans in Olympia. Charity was the beneficiary because those fans came out to see a very sentimental happening.

"Because of our age differences and the way the pro hockey draft works, it doesn't seem likely that I'll still be active by the time my sons are ready to play for the N.H.L.," he confided to a friend in mid-summer 1971.

Time for the Decision   131

Marty and Mark were certain now that hockey was to be their profession. They had proved they were good at it, and learning all the time.

Gordie expressed the hope that they would both go to college, something that had escaped him back in Canada. He had been noticing that college hockey was improving, getting very good in fact, but the boys still had a year or two to make that decision, one year for Marty and two for Mark.

Marty wanted to play in the Ontario Hockey Association that next season because "he had read somewhere that 90 percent of all players in the N.H.L. had played in the O.H.A. and he wanted to do the same thing," Gordie explained later.

"So we looked at the different teams to see what they could offer besides using Marty for a drawing card. We narrowed it down to four or five clubs just because of what educational facilities they offered. Then we turned it over to the boys. We gave them the car and told them to go see for themselves what the teams offered and where they wanted to play."

Marty liked Toronto, but he was also seriously thinking of St. Catherine's, also in Ontario, because Mark took a liking to St. Catherine's. The boys felt that wherever they went, they wanted to play on the same team, to be together.

Eventually, Mark decided he wanted to stay in the Detroit area one more year and play with his buddies on the Junior Red Wings, so Marty elected to sign with the Toronto Marlboros.

So, between the Gordie Howe Hockeyland rink, the Gordie Howe Hockey School, learning the insurance business, trying to help the boys determine their career direction, and frequent visits to the fast-growing cattle ranch at Grass Lake near Jackson, Michigan, it was a busy season for the Gordie Howes. Also, he was on the sports panel for Lincoln-Mercury, with friends such as baseball's Al Kaline, former Olympic great Jesse Owens, and others.

On top of that, a big, big honor for the Howes, Mark was selected as a member of the United States Olympic hockey team, the youngest member in the history of Olympics hockey.

Eventually the hectic summer, interwoven with some relaxing and fun-filled days at Bear Lake, came to an end as Labor Day approached—also the scheduled opening of the Detroit Red Wings training camp at Port Huron—the decision had to be made.

Gordie Howe made that decision as he had made every other, with frank honesty.

The day after Labor Day, Gordie played golf with son Mark at Plum Hollow Golf Club, which hosts the annual Gordie Howe Golf Tournament (since 1969) for the benefit of the March of Dimes.

That afternoon he confirmed his retirement: "Last year I felt like I was cheating," he said. "It seemed like I was making excuses all the time for the way I was playing. I just can't go on like that. I've got to be honest with myself and with the fans."

He spoke about the rib injury in the last season, and the constant pain in his wrists and one elbow. "My hand is better. The doctor has given me normal use of my left hand, but I'm not a one-handed hockey player. My legs didn't bounce back last year the way they used to. I remember saying they were hurt or that I was bruised. But those were just excuses. Lies, utter lies.

"I wasn't kidding myself. I only got 23 goals because of one hot streak. I didn't play very well. I could still execute the big play, but I couldn't do it often."

In the *Detroit Free Press,* Executive Sports Editor George Puscas wrote, in part, under an eight-column banner headline:

"Gordie Howe will play no more.

"The greatest player hockey has known, perhaps the

finest athlete of our time, has reached the end of a long and fabled career.

"He has quit, he said, because he feels he no longer can perform adequately and he does not want to embarrass himself or his team. There is more to it than that, but for the moment, hockey and Detroit must pause to acknowledge the end of an era and the withdrawal from the action scene of a most remarkable man.

"In his game and in his town he was in the image of Ty Cobb, skills unexcelled, his achievements unparalleled. Name them, the truly great ones who have graced the city's arenas—Cobb, Cochrane, Gehringer—a football player here and there—and none surpasses in his legend the Red Wings' No. 9.

"On the ice, he was an incomparable figure, big and husky with a long and effortless stride and a grace of movement that suggested laxity. Far from it. One does not play hockey for 25 years, when 20 is the longest anyone had ever gone, or score nearly 800 goals when 600 is the most anyone has ever scored, and be lax.

"His game was power. It was in his neck and shoulders and arms and wrists and in his legs, and though in the late years he rarely showed a trace of temperament, the newcomers knew his legend and made way for him.

"The classic picture of Howe is of his profile gliding toward goal, fending off pursuer with his free hand, pressing all the while on a wary goalie.

"He was at one time openly acknowledged as the toughest gut fighter in all of hockey, a reputation he spurned. . . . He was classic in his style as a complete team player, as a scorer and as symbol of his game.

"He has passed from hockey—and it is less a game because of it."

On Thursday, September 9, 1971, they made it official: Gordie Howe was now a vice-president of the Detroit

Hockey Club, with varied and far-reaching duties.

President Richard Nixon sent a telegram: "I wholeheartedly applaud the tremendous contributions you have made to the game of hockey, and to the lives of its many enthusiasts by your splendid sports career."

Detroit Mayor Roman S. Gribbs declared Thursday "Gordie Howe Day" with a proclamation that said: "Gordie Howe was more than a hockey star. He was a legend. It was not his unique talents alone that marked his greatness. His qualities as a man matched his unprecedented performance on the ice. If a city ever loved a sports hero, then Detroit has truly loved Gordie Howe."

Attending the luncheon at Olympia Stadium were two of his former coaches, Sid Abel, a former charter member of the "Production Line," and Tommy Ivan, his second coach, who followed the late Jack Adams. Red Wings owner Bruce Norris was there, as was the Howe family, Colleen and the four children, plus N.H.L. President Clarence Campbell, who was an N.H.L. "rookie" the same year as Gordie Howe (Campbell became president of the N.H.L. in 1946, the season Gordie started with the Red Wings).

Campbell said: "Never in the history of this game has there been such an obvious and dramatic loss by a single sport. This isn't intended to be a wake, but hockey has been fortunate to have Gordie. When he came into the league, hockey was a Canadian game and he's converted it into a North American game."

"My decision on retirement was based on many things," Gordie said, showing a typical lack of emotion. "It's a new life for me now and I'm looking forward to it. It started four or five years ago," he continued, admitting that he was "nervous as hell just talking about it. I came up with a bad year and I started to think about retirement. I've had wonderful success and it's been beyond the wildest dream I've ever had.

"I could play one more year and I could play very badly. But what good would that do when it could undo 25 years of work? My wife told me to play another year if I wanted, but she didn't want to see me suffer like I did last year when they should have benched me.

"Marty is leaving home to play junior hockey in Toronto and in another year Mark probably will be leaving, too. I want to spend some time with them before they get much older.

"Four or five years ago I asked Bruce Norris not to create a job here in Detroit for me, but to give me something where I can contribute."

The new job—probably paying about $75,000 for the dual insurance and hockey duties—would begin with the Red Wings training camp, where he would assist the coaches with the Red Wings and two farm clubs. Then he would work with the Fort Worth, Texas, and Tidewater, Virginia, farm clubs, making appearances and helping the players.

Gordie made it plain that he never would want to be a coach and had no designs on becoming a general manager.

Unfortunately, the duties with the hockey club were too vaguely defined. Newsmen and other knowledgeable observers had the "gut feeling" that trouble might well lie ahead for No. 9, if the Red Wings merely used him as window dressing to counteract or screen the very real front office problems.

Meanwhile, Gordie happily explored this new way of life as he beamed, "I'm learning so much that I don't have time to miss playing hockey."

Let's take a look at some of the awards he had received and some of the records he had engraved in N.H.L. history:

Lester Patrick trophy for outstanding service to hockey in the United States.

Most Hart trophies to the league's Most Valuable Player—six.

Most Art Ross trophies to league's highest scorer—six.

First active player, any sport, into Michigan Sports Hall of Fame.

Most career seasons—25.

Most career games, regular seasons—1,687.
Most games, including playoffs—1,841.
Most goals, regular seasons—786.
Most goals, including playoffs—853.
Most assists, regular seasons—1,023.
Most assists, including playoffs—1,114.
Most points, regular seasons—1,809.
Most points, including playoffs—1,967.
Most game-winning goals—122.
Most years in playoffs—19 (co-holder).
Most points in playoff final series—12 (1954-55).

Fastest goal from start of a playoff game—nine seconds (co-holder).

Most goals in a playoff semi-final series—eight (1948-49).

Most 20-or-more-goal seasons—22.

Most consecutive 20-or-more-goal seasons—22 (1949-50 through 1970-71).

Most 30-or-more-goal seasons—14.

Third in consecutive 30-or-more-goal seasons—five (1949-50 through 1953-54).

Third in 40-or-more-goal seasons—five.

Third in consecutive 40-or-more-goal seasons—three (1950-51 through 1952-53).

Third in points by a forward line in one season, the 1968-69 Detroit Red Wings "production line" of Frank Mahovlich, left wing (48), Alex Delvecchio, center (24), and Gordie Howe, right wing (42), total for the forward line, in 76 games—total points 114.

Second in penalty minutes—1,643 minutes in 1,687 games, 25 years (behind teammate Ted Lindsay with 1,808 minutes in 1,068 games, 17 years).

Second in penalty minutes, including playoffs, 1,861 (behind Ted Lindsay, 2,002 minutes).

Most All-Star games played—22 (in 25 years).

Most All-Star game goals—ten.

Time for the Decision 137

Most All-Star game assists—eight.
Most All-Star game points—18.
Most points in one All-Star game—four (co-holder).
Most All-Star game penalties—11.
Most All-Star game penalty minutes—25.

Gordie Howe's record with the Red Wings:

Season	Games	Goals	Assists	Points	Penalty minutes
1946-47	58	7	15	22	52
1947-48	60	16	28	44	63
1948-49	40	12	25	37	57
1949-50	70	35	33	68	69
1950-51	70	43*	43**	86*	74
1951-52	70	47*	39	86*	78
1952-53	70	49*	46*	95*	57
1953-54	70	33	48*	81*	109
1954-55	64	29	33	62	68
1955-56	70	38	41	79	100
1956-57	70	44*	45	89*	72
1957-58	64	33	44	77	40
1958-59	70	32	46	78	57
1959-60	70	28	45	73	46
1960-61	64	23	49	72	30
1961-62	70	33	44	77	54
1962-63	70	38*	48	86*	100
1963-64	69	26	47	73	70
1964-65	70	29	47	76	104
1965-66	70	29	46	75	83
1966-67	69	25	40	65	53
1967-68	74	39	43	82	53
1968-69	76	44	59	103	58
1969-70	76	31	40	71	58
1970-71	63	23	29	52	38
Totals	1,687	786	1,023	1,809	1,643

* led the league.
** tied leading the league.

The Detroit Red Wings' management problems continued into the new season—1971-72—while Howe stayed out of the hassles. When Ned Harkness was the coach and the players were ready to mutiny, general manager Sid Abel asked owner Bruce Norris if he, Abel, had the authority to fire Harkness; the reply was negative.

Abel, a former top player for the Wings, former coach and now general manager, resigned, holding a press conference at the Southfield Holiday Inn in which he blasted Harkness and others in the front office.

Harkness was moved upstairs to the general manager's office and former Wings player Doug Barkley was hired as coach. Now, early in the new season, Barkley resigned.

When Ned Harkness asked Gordie Howe to take over the coach's duties, at least on an interim basis, Howe declined. In an odd by-play, Harkness was quoted by newsmen as denying that he had offered the job to Gordie when Barkley's resignation was announced. But, when Howe was questioned, he frankly admitted having received the offer. This did not help Harkness' credibility with the sportswriters.

"Ned asked me right after Doug made up his mind to quit," Gordie explained, "but I had told everyone, including my wife Colleen, that I'd never take a coaching job when I resigned and I wasn't going to go back on my word.

"Even Bruce had said that I'd be foolish to take the coaching job. What do I need that for? We had a good coach in Doug Barkley and have a good one in Johnny Wilson. Johnny is going to turn this team around."

Unfortunately, Johnny Wilson, the 42-year-old former left winger for the Red Wings in the 1950s, didn't stay around as coach very long, either.

Here is an interesting little sidelight that points up what a big difference a couple of years makes when considering a person's reaction one day, then his reaction with the benefit of a couple more years' knowledge and experience.

Time for the Decision 139

Early in 1972, Gordie Howe was picked in the draft by the Los Angeles Sharks of the World Hockey Association, and he thought that was hilarious. "Oh, isn't that lovely," he said. "They're in trouble already if they want me to play. What's the name of that team that drafted me? Saints? Sharks? When I retired from the Red Wings last September, that was the end of my playing career."

Two and a half years later, Gordie Howe was beginning his second year in the World Hockey Association, with the Houston Aeros. The Los Angeles Sharks franchise had been moved to Detroit and was now the Michigan Stags of the W.H.A. The Stags' coach was Johnny Wilson, late of the Wings, and the Aeros, with the now famed Howe line, were playing an exhibition game against the Stags (nee Sharks) before a great crowd of Howe fans in Detroit's Cobo Hall.

However, back in early 1972, the Sharks were accused of using Gordie as a publicity gimmick. The Sharks' Gary Davidson acknowledged that they were not too serious: "It was more of a gesture because he's the world's most phenomenal player. I doubt if we'll be able to get him away from his job in the Detroit front office."

Gordie also reported that the Hamilton, Ontario, franchise of the W.H.A. had offered him a front office job, which he declined. "I'm happy where I am. I don't want to go anywhere."

Another honor came his way, a local one with much meaning, the Distinguished Sports Citizen Award for his work with the March of Dimes, and Gordie continued to answer press queries about his retirement experiences.

"You know what? I really love it. I had so much of the game that it doesn't bother me a bit not to be playing any more. There's no doubt in my mind that I made the right decision. This is a whole new career. I'm learning so much that I don't have time to miss playing hockey.

"I've seen all the Red Wings' home games. Normally I sit out in the crowd, although sometimes I go up in the press box. You certainly get a different perspective when you're not involved in the action.

"One thing I've learned to appreciate is the way Alex Delvecchio plays the game. He makes everything look so darned easy. It's a pleasure just to be able to sit and watch him." This about the man with whom Gordie had played so successfully side by side for such a long time.

About his work with the insurance agency and the Norin Co., he said, "When I retired from hockey one of my complaints was that I was spending too much time on the road. But in this job the trips are a lot shorter, they are to more interesting places and my wife, Colleen, can go with me most of the time. I try to stay in touch with Ned Harkness just about every day when I'm out of town on insurance business. And I get to Olympia every day that I'm in town, for meetings and to talk with Ned.

"One reason I don't care to coach is that I want my weekends free. We own a couple hundred head of cattle that are being raised on a farm outside of Jackson. I like to get up there as often as I can to watch my investment grow."

Howe continued to defend Ned Harkness, who was still being heavily criticized in the press and by the fans, whose banners read, "Darkness with Harkness" and things like that. "You have to spend time around Ned to really get to know him. I think he's a fine man and that, in time, he'll make the Wings a winner."

Gordie donned skates and pads once more for the Wings, in January, playing in the annual Old Timers' game, and had a ball.

Also in January 1972 the supposed pleasures of retiring from competition and entering the world of business took a bad turn—a couple of them—first an unfounded rumor broadcast by a television sportscaster that Howe was unhappy and was going to quit the Red Wings. He was unhappy, but had no thought of quitting.

"That would be the easy way out and I never gave it any

Time for the Decision   141

thought. Bruce wants me to be part of the team."

The unhappiness was triggered by a snafu in the insurance business plans. "When I retired, I had a dream that I would become involved in Bruce's insurance companies. That's what I had been preparing for the last few years of my playing career anyway.

"We worked for four months to build an office in Southfield [a Detroit suburb] and then last week I got a letter from Bruce saying that it would be another two years before I'd get to work in the insurance end and it really upset me. I've been working with Ned [Harkness] and [Executive Director Jim] Bishop on the hockey teams, but I was looking forward to the insurance work. This is what I've been building for."

A couple of years later, after it was all over, Gordie looked back on the problems of trying to serve two entities, the hockey club and the insurance business. "Once everything was all lined up for us to go somewhere on a promotion for insurance and then they turned around and on a day and a half notice they want me in Virginia for the hockey club, so I wondered what the heck's going on. I hardly knew where my orders were coming from, especially if we were supposed to be equal.

"They don't tell you anything, just bring you on and maybe you've been planning something and suddenly it's changed and when you've got a big family it takes a bit of planning. The little things add up. I say they're little, but they all add up. They pile up pretty big after awhile and I just, well the real thing was I wasn't learning. There wasn't much I could learn."

The change in insurance company plans hit like a bombshell. "I worked with a fellow named Bill Allison, who was almost like my direct contact. He was in Little Rock, Arkansas. Suddenly I noticed midway through the season that my checks all of a sudden were strictly from the hockey club and they weren't from the insurance company any more, so I phoned and asked what was the reason and they said they were having a big reorganization.

"Because of all the money being spent for legal fees in the reorganization into the Norin Co., it was easier for my money to come out of the hockey club. It didn't change the money at all. They were paying me almost more than I got when I was playing years and years."

Next, another rude awakening. "I just happened to find the annual report of the insurance companies and my name wasn't on it anymore. I had been a vice-president. They were planning a business meeting in Jamaica and Colleen and I were supposed to go. I phoned Bill Allison to find out what was going on and he didn't seem to know, so I phoned a fellow by the name of Lou Ricci and he didn't seem to know because I was now asking am I still with the company? Am I on the program at Jamaica? Finally, he says, 'Well, no, you are not on the program at Jamaica.'

" 'Well if I'm not on the program at Jamaica, it's a charity trip and I really don't need that because I have enough to do up here.' Then I phoned Bill Allison to find out what the heck was going on, only to find that, now, he was no longer with the company, either.

"Everything just added up to—you know, you are hung up in a closet until the hanger broke, and then you're in trouble."

Gordie Howe took the direct approach—to the boss man. "It took me a few days to get hold of Bruce and we set up a meeting in Miami for Tuesday [January 4, 1972]. I told Bruce I was unhappy. How do you expect I would feel if I'm not doing anything and don't feel involved?"

The outcome of that meeting: Gordie Howe was designated as the Wings' vice-president in charge of public relations. "I'm my own boss in this thing," he told newsmen on his return from Miami. "There's only one man to whom I have to report and that's Bruce Norris. If anyone wants me to do something, they'll have to come to me and then I'll only do it if I want to.

"I'm my own man now. Bruce has given me complete control of what I do and no one is going to interfere." The people to whom he referred were General Manager Ned Harkness, Executive Director Jim Bishop, and Olympia General Manager Lincoln Cavalieri. Harkness and Bishop were relatively new. Cavalieri had been with Olympia and the Red Wings for many years.

18

The Two Greatest Honors for an Athlete

"The most significant problem Gordie Howe has raised for the future of professional hockey in years to come is that there will never be another one like him."—from Beddoes *et al, Hockey! The Story of the World's Fastest Sport.*

Recognizing the validity of that observation, the Detroit Red Wings officially retired Gordie's No. 9 jersey at ceremonies Sunday, March 12, 1972, between the periods of the Red Wings and Chicago Black Hawks game, at center ice at Olympia Stadium.

They rolled out the red carpet for old No. 9, literally, with the Wings players lined up on one side and the Black Hawks on the other. Vice-President Spiro Agnew flew in from Washington, carrying a personal message from President Nixon. National Hockey League President Clarence Campbell flew in from Montreal. They were all there, politicians, civic leaders, former teammates, the press, radio and television, a hundred policemen and 14,291 paying customers who sang "'Cause if you're a Howe fan, you've got the very best!"

This gala ceremony was not the creation of the Wings' management, strange as that may seem. The scheduling, yes, but they had thought about a modest affair at center ice. Chuck Robertson, the 34-year-old head of Paddock Pools, a major sponsor of Junior Hockey and a close friend of the Howes, was asked to put the thing together. He started with President Nixon and never stopped.

"As the holder of the only black belt in golf, I'm pleased to honor my fellow athlete Gordie Howe," said Vice-President Agnew. "You know Gordie's wrist shot has been timed at 114.2 miles an hour. That's only slightly faster than the golf shot that I skulled Doug Sanders with at Palm Springs."

President Nixon's message to Gordie was: "When most men retire they are put on ice. But in your case there isn't a hockey fan in America who wouldn't want to put you on ice again to enjoy and savor the wizardry of your incredible hockey skills."

Among the many gifts was a painting of the famed Production Line of the 1950s—Gordie, Sid Abel, and Ted Lindsay.

The N.H.L.'s Clarence Campbell said, "The whole world of hockey owes him more than we can ever repay." Lindsay, Bill Gadsby, U.S. Senator Robert Griffin, and many others had their own words for No. 9. Then it came the turn of his arch rival, Bobby Hull of the Chicago Black Hawks.

Hull took a big wad of gum from his mouth to speak, then put it back as he decided to shake hands with Gordie, then took it out again to say, "I've played against the greatest of us all and I've enjoyed every high-sticking minute of it!" That brought down the house.

Bruce Norris announced that a scholarship was being established in the name of Gordie Howe, $1,500 each year, to go to a deserving student.

The Two Greatest Honors for an Athlete

Standing with Gordie was his wife Colleen, two sons Mark and Murray, and sister Cathy. Marty was absent because he was playing hockey that day in Toronto, but Gordie missed most his mother, who had died the previous summer. "If there was anything else that I wish now, it would be to have another Howe here with me."

As Bruce Norris accepted the No. 9 jersey, Gordie cautioned, "Don't wrinkle this because I've got a couple of boys who might wear it some day."

NEXT—the N.H.L. Hall of Fame!

They waived the three-year waiting rule to elect Gordie Howe to the Hall of Fame in his first season of retirement, along with Jean Beliveau of the Montreal Canadiens; Bernie "Boom Boom" Geoffrion, then coach of the Atlanta Flames; the late Harry "Hap" Holmes, a 1920s goalie for the Toronto Arenas and the Detroit Cougars; the late Hooley Smith of the Montreal Maroons and New York Americans in the 1920s and '30s, and Weston W. Adams, chairman of the board of the Boston Bruins.

First, the announcement was made at a luncheon in Montreal, and Gordie began to get suspicious. "I got an inclination of what was going to happen when I went down to Montreal for the luncheon where the new Hall of Famers were to be introduced, because they made a special attempt to make sure all of the new members would be there.

"But I didn't really think it would happen until the fellow congratulated me on making it." About their waiving of the waiting period rule: "As I see it, I infringed on the rules so many times in my career, maybe that's why they infringed on the rules now to get me in the Hall of Fame. For me, I'm glad they did and I can be there and enjoy it now."

For the official presentation, to take place in Toronto in August of 1972, Mrs. Carole Israel of suburban Birmingham, Michigan, sculpted a bronze statue of Mr. Hockey, to be presented to the N.H.L. Hall of Fame.

Actually, the work on the sculpture had been started a year earlier, at the time of his retirement from the ice, the idea of Detroiter Bob Steinberg.

The statue had been sculpted in wax, then cast in bronze. The timing could not have been better.

At the induction ceremony, Gordie was his usual nervous self when planted in front of a microphone: "After preparing myself 30 some years ago for this, I'm at a loss for words." He recalled the growing up on the Canadian prairie, saving pictures of N.H.L. players and hoping he might come close to their standards, and he talked about his family, his parents, his brothers and sisters, his wife and children.

"To say I made it alone would be a big lie. There were the Sid Abels, the Bill Gadsbys, the Red Kellys, the Ted Lindsays, the Alex Delvecchios."

Detroit News hockey writer Jack Berry recalled the day at Olympia Stadium "back in the '60s when Chuck O'Brien organized a 'night' for Howe. Gordie stood at center ice, choked up (the only time that happened on ice) and said, 'It's a long way from Saskatoon.'

"Yes it was," Berry continued, "and no one made the journey with higher style."

Marty Howe had recorded a successful year as defenseman for the Junior A team in the Ontario Hockey Association, the Toronto Marlboros. He was now 18 years old, about six feet tall and 180 pounds.

The younger Mark had missed much of the 1971-72 season with the Junior Red Wings of the Southern Ontario Junior Hockey League because of corrective knee surgery. He had played in nine games, scored five goals, and had nine assists. At Toronto, Marty's record was 56 games, seven goals, and 21 assists, with 122 minutes in the penalty box. He was proving aggressive like the old man. "I like the contact," he said.

For a while it was feared by the Howes that a sudden change in procedure by the O.H.A., in which they decided to

The Two Greatest Honors for an Athlete

draft from the Junior Red Wings after agreeing not to do so, would endanger the desire of the two boys to play together on the same team.

Gordie was bitter about what he felt was a double cross. "They not only passed a new rule, but they made it retroactive. "There's a lot of hockey potential in the Detroit area and they are just realizing it. They're trying to make the Detroit area a farm club to feed players to the O.H.A."

Mark Howe was drafted from the Junior Wings by the London Knights of the O.H.A., who in turn cashed in by trading Mark to the Toronto Marlboros for two players.

With Mark about to join his brother on the Toronto club, he sat down and made out a list of things he wanted before he would sign.

"First," Gordie said, "was that they wouldn't cut his hair and if they did they'd have to pay him $10,000. Last year, when Marty played with the Marlboros, they cut the new kids' hair as an initiation. Mark wants to keep his hair." Marlboro President Frank Bonello later assured Mark there would be no haircutting.

Mark also listed a requirement that they would introduce him to someone so he could play golf at some of the local clubs, and he asked for—get this—a team jacket.

"I told him to ask for that for good luck," admitted Gordie, remembering his first signing with the Red Wings and his demand for a team jacket that had been promised, but not delivered.

Gordie was quite proud that Mark did not list any money demands, just as his father never did.

Youngest son Murray was playing hockey regularly in the Detroit area and Marty and Mark were well on their own way to their professional hockey careers.

At Toronto, the 1972-73 season would see Marty, the defenseman, play in 38 games, missing part of the season when he became ill with mononucleosis, but scoring 11 goals, 17 assists and sitting out 81 minutes of penalties.

For Mark, his rookie year would be good, playing in 60 games, scoring 38 goals and 41 assists with 104 points for the season, one more than Dad's best year with the Wings. Mark was assessed 20 minutes in penalties. He was the point leader in the playoffs, with 26 markers.

ON THE ICE

A few years after he became the first active hockey player to receive the Lester Patrick Trophy as the man who contributed the most to hockey in the United States, Gordie Howe poses with the trophy.

Two famous No. 9s, Chicago's Bobby Hull (in white) and Detroit's Gordie Howe.

Gordie Howe goes one against three, battling two defensemen and the goalie as he moves to score another goal for the Detroit Red Wings.

Above: (l to r) Mark Howe, Gordie Howe, and Marty Howe. The boys were playing for the Roostertail-sponsored team in the Detroit junior league. *Below:* The first family of hockey—back row (l to r): Gordie, Mark, Colleen, Marty. Front row (l to r): Murray, Cathy.

(L to r) Mark, Gordie, and Marty Howe. The boys were playing for the Olympia Agency team in the Detroit junior league, maturing and building their reputations as future stars.

A 1967 poster of Gordie Howe.

1968

GORDIE

GORDIE MARTY

MARTY

MARK

World Hockey Association

The "Howe line"—Gordie (left), Marty, and Mark.

19

Out One Era and in Another

All conditions were so very right early in 1973—everything seemed to mesh at the same time, the good and the bad—to change the entire futures of several Howes and hundreds of other people, most for the better.

For Gordie Howe, the relationship with the Detroit Red Wings all started to come apart when the people in the front office bluntly told Gordie to keep his wife away from Olympia Stadium and the Junior Red Wings.

For years, Colleen Howe had been publicly recognized as the spark plug of the youth hockey operations, the one who had worked tirelessly, sold tickets, raised money, played chauffeur, counseled, guided, on and on and on. But those were happening in an earlier day with other people in charge of the Detroit Hockey Club.

The newcomers had traded away many of the old members of the team and the sportswriters had labeled many of the trades of the spite variety, cleaning house, getting rid of those who were there before the newcomers.

Now, apparently, Colleen Howe fell into that category.

Gordie said later, "I should have packed it up right then," but he didn't, because of that feeling that quitting was the easy way out.

He had been hurt personally when they had told him to stay away from the practice sessions, to stay out of the locker room, to stay off the ice. He was told that the coach, Johnny Wilson, wanted it that way. Johnny Wilson told him that Harkness had issued the order.

Gordie swallowed that affront, but when they attacked his wife, that was different. He became bitter, a complete reversal of his almost always before normal temperament.

"I may have disturbed a few people at the Olympia," Colleen recalled later. "I really don't know. It was never my intention to do so. I think that truly Gordie always did everything that he thought would count for the Red Wings and I always tried to act in the same fashion and whatever I did was to complement our family and our marriage and his career and so forth.

"So, if I did step on someone's toes and they didn't like it, I can't worry about that now. I have to do what I feel is right."

Gordie laughed as he recalled Colleen's dedication to the Junior Red Wings: "She believed so much in the Juniors and the Juniors were so strong—this is back when I was playing—that we [the Red Wings] would be practicing and she'd have the youngsters there and get impatient and say, about the Wings, 'Who are they, anyway? Get them off the ice and get the Juniors practicing!' She really believed in what she did."

Apparently the latter-day management didn't. Regardless, the storm clouds were black and Gordie Howe was becoming very unhappy. "I wasn't being utilized. I was making good money but I wasn't earning my money, so we kind of thought, kind of made plans that when we got something else going, we'd get away from there."

Out One Era and in Another   153

That something came in a phone call one day, early in 1973.

The World Hockey Association was completing its first season and on the Houston Aeros team, the head coach was a fellow named Bill Dineen, a forward for five years on the Detroit Red Wings, 1953-54 through 1957-58, a friend of the Howes, a teammate who had been their guest at home on several occasions.

The assistant coach was Doug Harvey, the veteran defenseman who had joined the Montreal Canadiens one year after Gordie joined the Wings. Later Harvey was with the New York Rangers, then for a short time in 1966-67 he was a teammate on the Red Wings.

Bill Dineen picks up the story: "I did have the opportunity of playing with Gordie back in Detroit for five years and the idea came to us that we might be able to draft the boys, Marty and Mark."

When did Gordie know what they had in mind? "About five minutes before they did it. Billy didn't even want to call me because he thought too much of me—as a player and a guy—to throw this at me that way, so he said, 'Doug Harvey, you do it,' so Doug phoned.

"Everything was going so super for us then (other than at Olympia) because we had this product and were pushing out into the agricultural business and we had just made a couple of big sales. Then I had been offered a contract more or less and had talked with Sears and they wanted me on their staff.

"Everything was going so nice and then Houston called about the boys and it was one more feather in the hat. We felt the boys were ready for the N.F.L., in fact, so we were in favor of Houston drafting them."

Bill Dineen: "The draft was on a Thursday night and on the following Tuesday morning I phoned Gordie because the one thing I wanted him to realize was that we didn't do the thing as a gimmick, that we were very serious about it. It sure wasn't an exhibition. Doug Harvey, our chief scout, had scouted Mark and Marty all through the O.H.A. playoffs. I went in to see Doug and he certainly didn't have to convince me of their ability.

"I explained that to Gordie and we talked on the phone for 15 or 20 minutes, talking about the boys. Just about the end of the conversation, Gordie said to me, just before I hung up, he said to me, 'How would you like a third Howe?'"

Gordie: "He never answered for a long time and I asked, 'Are you still there, Bill?'"

Dineen: "There was a considerable pause and then I said, 'That sounds like a great idea,' and we hung up.

"The first thing I did when he got off the phone was to phone the World Hockey Association office in Anaheim and we put Gordie on our protected list."

Many meetings later, Gordie Howe signed a four-year contract, reported at one million dollars, requiring him to play only the first year, followed by three years in management.

Gordie explained: "Colleen and I are splitting it. The four-year contract is close to a million dollars."

Marty and Mark both signed with Houston, reportedly four-year contracts, at $400,000 each. As Marty confirmed, "We're getting close to a million between us."

When Gordie told Bruce Norris that he was leaving the Red Wings and was going back into uniform with Houston, Norris came up with another offer, not too clear, that "the N.H.L. wants you to stay on and do public relations for them and for that we'll give you X number of dollars, but you'll have to do more than you've been doing."

That burned Gordie—hurt him that this was the way Norris had things figured. "I honestly think that someone [in the front office] probably led Norris to believe that I wasn't doing anything or wanted to do anything. There was the day that they tried to find me and raised all kinds of fuss because

I wasn't in town. Finally one of the secretaries, the one who did my work, told Harkness, 'If you'll look at the schedule in your own desk drawer, you'll see that you have him in Richmond, Virginia, today!' 'Oh,' he said.

"I don't know, whoever got that man's ears—when he listened—I don't know. They had to be telling him things, because Bruce was away from the picture himself."

Great athletes in their professional twilight years would do well to listen and profit from the temporary sad retirement experience of Gordie Howe.

"Nobody teaches an athlete how to retire! It's a problem," he warned, as he surveyed the almost aimless drift of his professional sports life those two years in semi-retirement. Faithful Gordie Howe watchers suffered as they witnessed the erosion of the spirit of their hockey hero.

Near the end of his playing career, Gordie said, "There were days I wished I didn't have to play. Practices were very hard for me. When you're near the end of it, you sit down and talk to yourself. You say, 'Where else can I earn that money doing something I like?' So you keep on.

"Sitting in the room when it's the fourth game in five nights, you're tired and you look across the room and see a young fellow dressing who wasn't even born when you first played the game. I once told Sid Abel, 'I can't stand that kid. Get him out of here!'

"Then I retired and when I went into the dressing room, everybody's talking about something about which I'm totally lost. Somebody tells a punch line and they all laugh and you don't have any idea what they are talking about.

"One of the guys asked me why I didn't come in more often and I said, 'Because I feel awkward in there.' He said, 'I know what you mean. When I'm hurt and miss a few games, I get the same feeling when I come back.'

"Then," Gordie said, "they told me to stay away from the locker room anyway.

"I don't blame Bruce Norris. I have to thank him for

trying. He justified our friendship by getting me a very good lucrative job and all I could do was sit there and do nothing.

"When you're hired, you generally like a man to tell you what to do. Johnny Wilson [one of the ex-coaches] said he was told not to put me on the ice because I liked to fool around a lot and I would just hold up the tempo of his practices.

"Then I was told by another party that it was Johnny who didn't want me on the ice. Then, something was said in terms of that Alex Delvecchio didn't want me in the room.

"All those stories. My God. Can you imagine that after 27 years?"

The long-time friendship of Ted Lindsay and Gordie Howe began to unravel when the first rumors broke that Howe might be planning to resign all connection with the Red Wings, and it burst into a full-blown rupture when Howe signed with the World Hockey Association.

The split hurt the sensitive Howe because Lindsay had been his first and his longest-running and closest friend in professional hockey. "I should be mad at Ted because of some things he has said. I don't know what the heck he does it for. He was saying something like why should I be unhappy with the Red Wings when they paid me so good and treated me nice.

"I'd have liked to put him in the same position and see what would have happened. He was a hot-headed individual and he and Jack Adams were so much alike that they hated one another. It looks like he was trying for an N.H.L. manager's job somewhere and he wanted to prove to somebody where his alliances were, so that seems why he would use somebody like this."

Lindsay has been a television broadcaster for the N.H.L. games for a few years, and there was some talk that he might be considered for the Red Wings managerial spot if Ned Harkness left.

"I don't think he will ever get that," Gordie explained,

"because, very frankly, Ted came out very strongly on a newscast tape that he was going to have it this way and that way [if he became the manager] and when a man's got seventeen million wrapped up in a club like Bruce Norris has, you are not going to tell him how to spend his money.

"Ted knocked me before with the hockey school. Someone was saying that he was going to attend the Gordie Howe Hockey School and Lindsay asked him what he wanted to do that for because 'you'll never see Howe there. He's never there.' That's not true, I was there every day, for from six to eight hours every day. Well, he's been a little that way. He's done other little things throughout our meetings.

"You know, he took a run at Sid Abel as soon as Abel was out of the picture with the Wings. I don't know why he does it. In a case like this I could care less."

The Ted Lindsay and Gordie Howe split widened after the first Howe season at Houston, 1973-74, and Gordie recalled: "Ted voiced his opinion very strongly against the W.H.A. and that an old man of 46 could be leading the league. He said it's a crime and indicated how bad the league was."

Still a year later, Ted Lindsay publicly acclaimed Howe's greatness with the N.H.L. when he was asked his opinion whether Bobby Orr is the greatest hockey player.

Published in the May 1975 issue of *Sport* magazine, Lindsay said: "Gordie Howe is still the greatest all-round player. You can't argue with his record. He played 25 years in the N.H.L. and has the most goals, most assists and most points.

"If Orr lasts anywhere close to that long, he'll rewrite the record book. Howe was not as advanced as Orr at this stage of his career. His growth came late.

"Both of them are reactors; they can do whatever the situation demands. Gordie was more physical. He worked those corners like a riot cop. He didn't go out of his way looking for trouble, but if trouble found him, he quietly took care of it. He'd wait until he caught the guy away from the play, and you'd look around and the guy suddenly would be out cold on the ice.

"Orr accelerates better, but Gordie's stride was deceivingly easy. Their slap shots are close. Howe had a better wrist-snap shot.

"Both of them can make the big play spontaneously. . . . Against Chicago once, [Howe] was coming in on goal and being checked from behind, on his right side. He switched his stick to his left hand, shot and scored."

As *Sport* magazine summed it up: "Lindsay, of course, played 12 years with Howe in Detroit and could be biased."

Lindsay may have "taken a run at" Gordie Howe and the W.H.A. to prove his loyalty to his broadcasting meal ticket, the N.H.L., but he still remembered and cast his vote for No. 9 as the best.

Even while holding contracts worth about two million dollars—a half million each for the next quartet of winters—planning the move from the Detroit area was a traumatic experience for the Howes, senior and junior.

"I have regrets about leaving Detroit because of the friends we made over the years and the wonderful way people have treated us and I suspect my wife Colleen is having some second thoughts," Gordie said, "but I have no regrets about the other place." It was almost as if he didn't even want to mention the name of Olympia Stadium.

Soon after the Howes would leave town, this summer of 1973, they would be back, the three male members in uniform as the W.H.A. scheduled two pre-season exhibition games in Cobo Hall, back to back, first with the Minnesota Fighting Saints, then with the Los Angeles Sharks. You remember the Sharks, they were the folks who drafted Gordie Howe the year before. Of course, no one knew it then, but this was the same team that would later move to Detroit as the Michigan Stags.

Anyway, back to 1973, as the Howes prepared to leave

their town. Detroit Red Wings assistant manager Jim Skinner also angered the usually unflappable Howe. "I'm surprised at Skinner. I've known him for years. We started out with the Wings together. Now the other night he was on radio and commenting about the Aeros' coming exhibition games here and said, 'Let the fans go down and see them and they'll realize they [the Aeros] just play minor league hockey.'

"I think the hockey in the W.H.A. is as good as the N.H.L. I don't know about Skinner, I suspect his head is now as fat as his stomach. You know, I've had about three letters criticizing me for leaving the Wings. And once a man stopped me and questioned me about leaving and I told him my reasons and he said, 'Why did you wait so long?'

"Do you know how much my last paycheck was for? Fifty-one dollars! I couldn't believe it. For some reason they always paid me through the [Olympia] Travel Agency. I'm not sure why. Anyway, when I quit, they took out for all the recent plane trips I had made for the Wings and deducted them from my paycheck. Some of the trips had been on my own business, but everywhere I went I represented the Wings. It was pretty cheap."

It was obvious that feeling was running deep on both sides. The people from the Red Wings, and with N.H.L. affiliations, were feeling threatened. For years, theirs was the only game in town. Now this upstart W.H.A. had snatched away the biggest name in N.H.L. hockey—not only Gordie, but the two younger Howes they had been counting on to come along and keep the dynasty going.

The entire chain of events that had led to Gordie Howe's retirement from the ice, his unhappy year-plus in the front office, his final Red Wings resignation and the move to the rival W.H.A., was so predictable—all but the W.H.A. chapter—that if you wrote it as a plot you'd never even come close to winning an Oscar or an Emmy.

Sid Abel, veteran player, member of the establishment,

is the general manager and coach; new coach is brought in from outside, Ned Harkness, with championships at two colleges, but never in the N.H.L.; the team continues to skid and the players are in revolt; Sid Abel wants to fire coach, but owner says no; Abel resigns and the newcomer coach becomes general manager; other establishment coaches come and go.

Gordie Howe retires and is saluted far and wide as the greatest of all time, a local hero of tremendous proportion, but he is of a professional hockey generation before Harkness. The press, radio and television praise Gordie and snipe at Harkness.

Bruce Norris knows he owes much to Howe, so he sets him up in a good paying job with a title, but thinly defined duties, responsibilities, and authority. If ever an arrangement was devised to fractionalize an organization, this was it.

Gordie could have taken his ample paychecks and relaxed and said the hell with it, but he is not that kind—he wanted to work, to earn his dough.

Perhaps the newcomers didn't know what to do with him, perhaps didn't care, perhaps even wished he would fade away. When they tried to casually retire his famous No. 9, a tradition they felt should be followed, it became such an important occasion the Vice-President of the United States flew in especially, from Washington, with a personal message from the President.

Gordie Howe's image was a whole lot bigger than the recent management, a condition that even in the best of times does not induce harmony. Howe tried to find work to do, but as he said, "We were all supposed to be equal." That may have been the problem. The big man did not exercise his authority, did not define the demarcation.

The frustrated Gordie Howe summed it up with the classic description:

"They gave me the mushroom treatment. That's when

Out One Era and in Another 161

they keep you in the dark and every once in a while open the door and throw in some more manure on you!"

For the record, here is what happened with the Red Wings after Howe's resignation and departure.

November 7, 1973, 41-year-old Alex Delvecchio was told that he was no longer a player on the Detroit Red Wings—he was the new coach.

Gordie Howe, asked for his assessment of his old linemate in the new job, predicted better things in the future for the Wings. "You know it's not the whip you carry that makes guys want to play. I think that's where I was always at odds in my thinking with the people who were running the club in Detroit. I think a happy club is important. Sometimes guys will play really better than their ability if the excitement is there. That means they've got to be happy."

The Wings won their first game under the new coach, beating the North Stars 4 to 2 at Minneapolis, but they finished their 1973-74 season sixth in their Eastern Division, with 29 victories, 39 losses, and 10 ties.

In the meantime, Ned Harkness resigned as general manager and Delvecchio was knighted to handle both jobs, coach and general manager.

The Wings continued to be a losing club, but the situation was much more calm. The sportswriters and sportscasters gave moral support to Delvecchio.

For the 1974-75 season, the Wings finished fourth in the new five-team Wales Conference of the Norris Division, winning 23, losing 45, and tying 12 games. Management announced they finished the year in the red by $300,000, but also announced that Delvecchio would be back as general manager and coach.

Bruce Norris said: "It's been a difficult year and it's been frustrating that we haven't been able to put things together. Alex took over a situation with a lot of problem areas and he's done a fine job."

Still later, Delvecchio was promoted to general manager and Doug Barkley was hired as coach. Upward and onward toward 1975-76.

With the Red Wings smoothing out their problems, things turned better for Ned Harkness, also, in January 1975, when he was hired by Union College in Schenectady, N.H. to develop ice sports on an intramural and intercollegiate level and to manage its new ice rink, being built at a cost of a million and a half dollars.

Ned's father, Bill "Pop" Harkness, had coached varsity hockey and lacrosse at Union from 1929 to 1940, when the college dropped hockey as an intercollegiate sport. Now, Ned Harkness was designated once again to put together a varsity hockey program for the college.

Harkness had won national collegiate hockey championships at Rensselaer Polytechnic Institute and later at Cornell University before going to the Red Wings.

"This is where I belong," said Harkness. "It's like coming home. My Dad coached here for 12 years and I watched my brother graduate from Union and my kids were born about 12 miles away. I've spent a lot of enjoyable years in college athletics.

"I don't have any animosity toward the Red Wings," he continued. "The Wings are still my favorite team. I have a lot of regard for Bruce Norris and Alex Delvecchio. I feel I did a good job, especially in a lot of areas invisible from the fans and press. I improved the farm system, I improved the scouting system and I put the operation on a businesslike basis."

Harkness blamed pressures from the press and fans for driving him out of the Red Wings, but said some of the blame for the Wings' failures should go to the players.

"They're the ones who put on the skates and go out on the ice to play the game. But they don't have the great incentives they used to. The big salaries and the players' association have deteriorated their incentives."

Detroit hockey fans could only wish Harkness well in his new job. Mark Beltaire summed it up in the *Detroit Free Press:* "Now that Ned Harkness is back in college hockey where he belongs, a man recalled the reaction of Dr. William Keast, former president of Wayne State University, when Harkness was brought to Detroit as general manager of the Red Wings. Keast and Harkness had known each other at Cornell, where Harkness was hockey coach, leading to Keast's appraisal: 'He's a fine man, but he's about as qualified to manage the Red Wings as I am to run the Detroit Tigers.' "

20

A Look Back—
A Look Ahead

After you have lived in one place for 27 years, and you are planning to leave, the emotions run deep and you find yourself looking back, remembering the good times.

"I lived in the Detroit area for 27 years, but if you count the first year in Galt and the second year when I was with the Ontario club, the ties were to Detroit, so it's been close to 30 years," Gordie said, as he relaxed at his summer place on Bear Lake.

"When Colleen and I were first married, we lived in a little place on Stawell in Detroit [the near northwest side] in what they call the Joy Road-Wyoming district. We were just on the inside corner and real close to Colleen's home on Kentucky, at Kentucky and West Chicago, or Wyoming and West Chicago, they are all close there. We weren't too far from where she was born and that's how we got going in that area.

"Marty and Mark were born when we lived on Stawell.

Later we moved out to Lathrup Village [northern suburb] because the boys were getting a little maturity in age. Cathy was born when we lived at Lathrup, and Murray, too.

"At Lathrup Village we were able to build a rink right out in the front yard. It took a lot of hard work. We put a screen on the bottom and put up some sideboards, then filled it with water. It worked pretty good. One winter we had a tremendous cold winter and it held up pretty well and Cathy did a little figure skating. She enjoyed it, but I think she's more musically inclined. She's pretty good on the organ and she's got art, but she doesn't really know what to do."

Cathy herself said, "I haven't decided. I can play the organ and piano and have taught myself how to use them. I haven't taken any lessons or anything." She is attending high school and is aiming at college.

Growing up in Lathrup Village was interesting and, as Marty explained, "Once in a while Dad got mad at us when were were younger, but he was gone quite a bit and Mother, she kept us in a straight line."

Colleen agreed that for a mother to handle a couple of rugged growing boys might be a problem, especially as they grow as big or bigger than she is, but explained, "Yes, I think that has to happen, but by a certain age the die has to be cast or the lessons have to be learned. Meanwhile it's respect. We tried to teach mutual respect. We respected our children a great deal and they know that. We, in turn, expect them to respect us."

Speaking about her father's traveling so much, Cathy said, "In a way, sometimes it was different [from other families], but we were together in the summers and I guess you don't realize you are any different because it was that way all our life, because he was always going away, but always coming back."

With young Murray, the youngest, "No, it didn't make any difference, because in the summers he was around okay. In the winters he was away a lot, but as long as he was around in the summers, it was okay!"

In 1972, about the time of the retirement from the ice, they bought a larger house in Bloomfield Hills, another affluent northern suburb of Detroit. Came time for the move to Houston and Gordie said, "We were wondering what we were going to do with it because you can't leave a house vacant today, and along came some people who wanted to rent a home in that particular area and that worked out perfect.

"The boys asked if we were going to sell the home in Bloomfield Hills, but we'll keep it for a while and see what happens. And they they said, 'What about the cottage [at Bear Lake]. If you're going to sell it, we'll buy it.'

"No, we'll stay there in the summer. That was a dream, even though it's only a one-month-in-a-year deal."

What about leaving friends behind, when making a big move?

"Hockey players are like gypsies. You are friends for eight months, then some are gone and you never see them again. The people I think you become close to are the people on the outside.

"In hockey, take Sid Abel. He used to be the captain of the club and we used to go to his place [in Gordie's early years with the Wings]. It was the only place I knew. From where we lived, near the rink, on Dexter out to Sorento, we used to run out that way and come back the same way or get lost.

"But I loved to go and fish and—I guess you would call it—simpler things and Sid loved the horses and he liked to play cards a little bit—well, a sort of different environment. I played for many years with the Kellys, the Lindsays, the Pavelichs—well, you know them, but maybe they don't like the things you like and as soon as the hockey season ends they go their way and you go yours.

"That's why I used to enjoy going to the Red Wing Alumni games and the summer meetings and playing some of the hockey games and having fun with the guys.

"But it is the people outside that you are closer friends

with. The family had a long talk about moving to Houston and we all agreed that to be a friend of this family you don't have to be on the doorstep all the time. If we see someone only twice a year it doesn't mean he is less a friend. That's not how we judge friends.

"The way we look at it, we were not leaving friends in Detroit. They still are friends and I hope they always will be. And we feel that here we have the opportunity to make new friends, to add to the list."

There was a lot of kidding about "Howe-ston" and "howe-dy" and things like that, but the traumatic experience, the real feeling of doubt, especially for Colleen, came with trying to make the decision about young Murray, then 13, whether he would go to Houston or stay in Bloomfield Hills.

Murray went to Houston with the family during the summer, attended some hockey meetings and practices, but elected to remain in Detroit.

"It was a terribly difficult decision for us," Gordie said, "but it was the only fair thing for Murray. In Houston, there is some junior hockey, but not on the scale of Michigan and nearby Canada. In Houston, he might have been able to play a few games a season. In Michigan he would be playing 100 games, and against much better players. There are 30,000 registered hockey players in Michigan, only 500 in Houston.

"His two older brothers had that opportunity just naturally, just because we were living there, and it would have been so very unfair to Murray to force him to give up what he had been working for so many years, something he dreamed about as I had and as his brothers had."

Arrangements were made for Murray to live with the Howes' close friends, the Chuck Robertsons. He was the fellow who brought Spiro Agnew and everyone to the official retirement party for the No. 9 jersey.

They worked out a partial custody arrangement and planned to keep in touch by phone and to spend as many

A Look Back—A Look Ahead 169

holidays and vacation times together as possible. The whole family spent the summer of 1973 together, in Houston or Bloomfield Hills or at Bear Lake.

"We told Murray it was his decision to make," Colleen said. "The Robertsons are old friends and Murray knew them and their family very well. We took our time about making the decision, but I told Murray that it's always better to have a decision that is reversible, like this one, when he could always decide to go to Houston."

As time passed, the plan did work out well. Murray continued to play hockey and to learn and advance. They phoned every week, Murray tore out stories about the Red Wings and mailed them to Houston, and they visited when they could, in either direction.

This is a very close family, and they made it plain that it will take more than 1,337 miles to affect that relationship.

When Marty and Mark Howe arrived in Houston for the official signing of their contracts with the Aeros, the teenagers were met at the airport and driven in a limousine to a plush suite in an exclusive hotel, in sharp contrast with their Dad's arrival at the Red Wings tryout camp, with a five dollar bill in the pocket of a new suit, both given him by the Wings' scout.

Obviously they would probably have not been there at all, certainly not with $400,000 or so contracts apiece, if it were not for the fact that their father was the greatest hockey player in the world. However, they had learned their skills well. In fact, they were better and more qualified rookies than he had been. They had the benefit of watching and learning from the master and his friends, and they had come along in an era of big-time sports affluence.

How does Gordie Howe feel about young hockey players (other than his relatives) receiving big contracts, like $150,000 a year or so? "Well, one thing I like about it, to be honest, is that—say if I had retired after 18 or 20 years in hockey, I would have had a little financial problem. We would not have had the things we have now and wouldn't have been invested in the things we have."

It was not until Gordie Howe's 23rd, 24th, and 25th years in the N.H.L. that he was being paid the big salary—$75,000 and $100,000.

"I think the boys should work for their money—and I know my two are working hard for their salaries—but now these young people, new in hockey, no matter who they are, don't have to be worried about their future [as he and his era were]. With proper guidance they can get investments going for them. We have the boys spread out in banking, cattle, apartment buildings."

Not only does Gordie especially appreciate the financial good fortune that has befallen his family, but he wants to see other young players better off than he was at their age.

As a boy, he used to listen to the hockey games on the radio and think about someday being with those big names, being one of them.

"There was a great name in hockey, Mel Hill, and when I was a young fellow about nine, he used to drive by our house in a great big convertible, sitting proud as a peacock, and that was a professional hockey player. I think that did it. I used to dream about it.

"I'd get the Eaton's catalog and I'd say, 'Mom, when I make it, you're going to have this and this and this,' and I'd have them all circled. I was pretty good on my math, because I used to add it all up. That was my big dream, which did come true, thank heaven. That's why I feel somebody upstairs likes me.

"After Colleen and I were married I was able to buy my folks the home that Dad lives in yet. I built the kitchen cupboards, and much to my surprise—that's been 20 years ago—they look as good as ever except the knobs are beaten up a little."

After they were married, the Howes spent their summers in Saskatoon. Colleen recalled, "The first two summers we lived in a one-room cottage with no running water. Then Marty was born, and needless to say, with no running water, you have no hot water. In order to do diapers and things, Gordie would go to the tennis club, which wasn't too far away, and bring hot water in pails in the trunk of the car. Those first years, Gord scrimped and saved and even had cardboard in his shoes until he was able to buy the house [for his mother and dad].

"Ted Lindsay had talked about coming out to Saskatoon in the summer, the year before he bought the house. Gord was scared to death that Ted or one of the other players would come to Saskatoon and find out his parents had an outhouse and no inside plumbing.

" 'What will I do?' he worried. He shouldn't have felt that way, but he had been in some homes in Detroit that were really nice and he didn't want his mother and dad to ever feel that they didn't have a good house."

The move to "Howe-ston" was made so much easier by the helpfulness and friendliness of the Houston Aeros people, Irv Kaplan, chairman of the board, Jim Smith, president and general manager, and others.

They found a new house, a big one, with space for a swimming pool and putting green, and the Aeros maintain a team membership at a golf club for the players and their families.

The hospitality was so great that Colleen phoned her friend Janet Popiel, wife of Poul Popiel, a former Detroit Red Wings teammate and an Aero from the beginning, and Colleen asked, "When is the bubble going to burst?"

"Never," said Janet. The previous year with the Aeros was the happiest year she and Poul had ever spent in hockey. She said Poul would do anything for that organization.

For Gordie, there was another reason to be grateful. "We always knew that the boys would leave home, but now, because of what the Houston Aeros have done for us, where the boys play hockey is at home."

"Moving to Houston came about so suddenly," Gordie

said. "As you know, I had just about made up my mind to leave the Red Wings organization anyway. That was getting worse all the time, and there were times when I had to shake myself and ask just what kind of people I was working with. So I was ready to go.

"Then Sears was talking about me going with them, we had the cattle ranch and there is a company in Ypsilanti called Silo Guard that makes a product the farmer adds to his silage and it prevents leakage. The Silo Guard greatly reduces the loss and the business was just taking off. We had made some good sales and it looked like I could go on the road and make more than I was making with the Wings.

"So I was preparing to go out and do the farmers some good and the family some good, when Doug Harvey called, then a couple days later Bill Dineen called."

"This was what the boys had worked for and they could break in on the same team. They had worked hard for it. Marty had a bone broken under his right eye and they had to go in with a wire and lift the bone back into place and turn it correctly. Mark had had a knee operation and a shoulder separation."

"Then when the Aeros asked Gord to play too," Colleen added, "it became a real family affair."

The first day of school in Houston was a rough one for young Cathy. The school was big, she had no friends, she missed Bloomfield Hills.

This changed the next day, however, when the girl sitting across the aisle from Cathy asked the teacher, "Do you know that the Howes of the Houston Aeros just moved in right down the street from me?"

"Yes," said the teacher, "and that girl across the aisle from you is Cathy Howe." That was the ice-breaker that led to many friendships.

When Gordie, Marty, and Mark first went to Houston to talk, "the people here said to take a day and look around and relax and we'll talk tomorrow. The next day we went to lunch and the owners were there. One came down from Dayton, Irv Kaplan came back from a California trip just to be with us. That gave us a warm feeling right off the bat. And it is apparent, they feel the same way about all the athletes, not just the Howes."

21

Career Number Two

The 1973-74 season for the Houston Aeros of the World Hockey Association opened with the usual string of exhibition games, at home and away, with two scheduled back to back in Detroit's municipally owned Cobo Hall, obviously not on the Bruce Norris-owned Olympia ice.

Gordie Howe was coming home, this time to play professional hockey alongside his teenage sons Marty and Mark. The games were against the Minnesota Fighting Saints Monday, October 8 and against the Los Angeles Sharks Tuesday, October 9. It was the Sharks who originally drafted Gordie Howe, or attempted to do so. Later the Sharks would become the Michigan Stags, with Cobo as their home ice, and later still they would fail in Detroit and go to Baltimore, and, unfortunately, fail again.

But, on these October nights, Detroit sportsdom welcomed the Howes back home and the Howes were delighted to be returning so soon after leaving.

On the eve of the first game, Gordie admitted, "I'll have a little more weight on my shoulders. It's not that I want to show anybody, to get back at Olympia or anything like that. It's just that I want to do well and by that show Detroit my appreciation for all that it's been to me and my family. These games in Detroit will be appreciation games."

At the beginning of the 1973-74 season, Gordie stated that he would also be back for a second season with the Aeros, an announcement that surprised those who felt his first year would be mostly tokenism, cashing in on the Howe name. It also surprised those who knew better, knew that Gordie would only give his best. It surprised them because of its advanced timing. Why say, now, that he would be back next year when he didn't even know how this year was going to go?

Gordie had good reason to make that decision, but it would be a year before he would reveal the reason.

On the eve of the home opener, as mentioned earlier, Gordie lay in traction in a Houston hospital, suffering the pains of a sprained back. "Oh, no! How can I go on like this?" he asked himself over and over. So many old friends were coming in from Detroit. He would not embarrass them or himself or his family or the Aeros or the Houston fans. He would play and play well.

It matters little that the Aeros lost that home opening game, because they went on to win the championship in their Western Division, with a record of 48 victories, 25 losses, and five ties, the best showing in the 12-team World Hockey Association.

Gordie Howe was named the Most Valuable Player in the W.H.A., Mark Howe was honored as Rookie of the Year, and Marty Howe received kudos as a coming defenseman star in pro hockey.

Gordie was third in points, playing in 70 games, scoring 31 goals, 69 assists, and earning an even 100 points. For a while, it appeared that he was on his way to winning the scoring championship, but he broke a bone in his foot, late in the season, missed a few games—eight, actually, all season—and had to settle for third in the standings.

Mark Howe was 14th in the W.H.A. scoring list, with 76 games, 38 goals, 41 assists, and 79 points. Defenseman Marty Howe played in 73 games, scored four goals, had 20 assists and 24 points, and was incarcerated in the penalty box for 90 minutes, almost double the 46 minutes assigned to Gordie.

With the Western Division championship tucked away, they moved through the playoffs to beat Bobby Hull's Winnipeg Jets in four straight games, then they captured the Minnesota Fighting Saints four games to two, then winning the finals against the Chicago Cougars in four games, 3 to 2, 6 to 1, 7 to 4, and 6 to 2, to win the Avco World Cup, the W.H.A.'s answer to the Stanley Cup.

Mark Howe was second in playoff points, with nine goals and 10 assists, 19 points. Gordie was sixth with three goals and 14 assists and Marty scored one goal and had five assists for six points.

Gordie and Mark were both selected for the W.H.A. All-Star team.

For the Aeros, the Howes proved to be a bonanza, as attendance almost doubled in the 9,300 capacity Sam Houston Coliseum and on the road the Aeros were drawing the largest gates in every visiting stadium.

Looking back on that first season, Gordie said, "I don't know, but I guess all of us have a little bit of ham in us and I had to enjoy those tremendous fans. They are not as sophisticated in their knowledge of the game as the Detroit fans, but they are caught up with the efforts put forth by the players.

"For instance, it's the normal thing when blocking a shot from a point, if you're close enough you just fall to the ice and let the other side go by you. Once, when I fell and blocked a shot and Mark quickly picked it up and dropped it out of the end, it was the funniest thing, there was a standing ovation—for blocking a shot, a standing ovation!

"This is the excitement that prevails and it is handed down so sometimes when you get aches and pains, well you don't even realize it.

"One night very early in the season, I said to Ted Taylor, the captain of the Aeros, 'My left side is really sore,' and he said, 'As soon as you hear the crowd, it will be gone.' "

What about the severe arthritic problem in both wrists? "Well, Doctor Bailey in Ann Arbor had told me that over the two-year span when I wasn't playing there would be a certain amount of growth, which would give the wrists support. I found out that both of the wrists hurt, but there was no real—what I would call severe—pain such as I was going through before, when after a game I had to hang that thing over my head to get any relief.

"This year, when we didn't have a game, we'd practice in the morning and go back and practice at night and other than a little stiffness it didn't bother me."

Often after a night game at home, Gordie would be out in the swimming pool at midnight, relaxing and chasing the aches and pains. He also played a lot of golf.

After a game, Marty and Mark are long gone with their young teammates. Gordie dresses slowly. "I'm tired."

Later, looking back, he concluded, "It was much more, much better than we expected. At first the two boys and I traveled back and forth to the rink and I looked at them and they were a little concerned and I said to myself, 'I really don't know if I have made the right decision.'

"All of a sudden it crowned more or less and I started feeling good, and the happiness of seeing the boys achieve. Marty didn't win an award, but if friendship is called an award, he got a lot of awards.

"Mark got into the scoring column in a hurry and he said, 'Okay, now stop worrying about me and get one on your own.' I'll admit I choked up a bit when he got that first goal. I was on the ice at the time, in fact I was involved in it, which I kind of liked.

"The one I remember, the defenseman, Marty, I felt he has to get a goal somewhere along the line. He had been hitting the goal posts, the goal tender kicks his right leg and the puck hits the left one and it's not going in.

"On this play, I carried the puck wide to my right because I saw a set of blue legs—the blue and white colors of the Aeros—coming up behind me, so when the opposing defenseman pulled over, I just slid it back and he ran me wide behind the net, and just then the net bulged about a foot and a half from my head.

"I pulled back and I said, 'Great. That's the kid's 20th.' I thought it was Mark's 20th goal, and then I looked around and saw the biggest smile you ever saw on Marty. I certainly thoroughly enjoyed that. I enjoy every game, even if we lost. You don't like to lose, but there is a certain excitement involved."

There have been some fights. Mark said, "I don't worry about him. He's big enough; he can take care of himself. I'm the smallest of the three, about five feet 10½ and 185, but he's always there to back me up. He can handle the tougher guys, and Marty's on the other side."

Gordie had a laugh recalling a night that Marty came up to protect the old man. "There was a goon on the other side—I wouldn't say he is a hockey player, he just gets out there on the ice and causes trouble. We were on a face-off and this guy is opposite me and Marty skates up and says, 'Get back in my position!'

"I asked him, 'What are you talking about?' and he says, 'Get back, I want at him.' I wasn't going to stand there and argue in front of 10,000 people, so I moved back to Marty's position and thank heavens the puck went thataway and there was no altercation. Marty was so mad at the guy he wanted a go at him."

There was a hassle in Cleveland one night when a heckler behind the Aeros' bench became what Coach Bill Dineen felt was too loud and too abusive, picking on several of the players, so Dineen asked the heckler to be a little more quiet.

One thing led to another and Dineen wound up in the stands, with Gordie right behind. "I was just going to the old boy's rescue," Gordie explained. "I looked up and he had problems so I just went to help him."

Mark said, "We all went up there. I got mad because a policeman had Dad. He had Dad's arms and anybody could have got to him. Marty and I got on the policeman and took him off my Dad, and then we went to help Bill out."

Gordie agreed that things can get rough in Cleveland at times. "One day someone was making up names for teams, like the Los Angeles Smogs, the New York Muggers, the Detroit So and Sos and when he got to Cleveland, all he could think of was the Cleveland Cleavers."

On another subject: "Sometimes I get thinking that with Mark we get the headlines, the fact that we get some goals, but at one time through the season, I think that Marty was the best man on the Aeros in a period of about a month's span.

"He got to the point where, in the Three-Star selection, there's generally a gift goes along with it and Marty had two of them hanging in his closet before the younger brother and the old man got even one.

"They've both been complimented all year, but what was really great, we were two men down and I was one of them in the penalty box, and Dineen put the two kids and Poul Popiel on the ice and they not only held their own, but scored a goal while two men short, so that to me was great. I had trouble getting out of the penalty box after that."

Gordie feels the weather in Houston works to the advantage of the Aeros. "I definitely noticed the heat when I first got there. A visiting club coming in, I feel sorry for them sometimes, because it gets tremendously hot, but we get accustomed to it and then we go north and getting into nice, cool, dry weather, we feel so refreshed we feel like skating all day."

Bill Dineen was talking about Marty Howe: "We thought Marty was a good hockey player, but we had no idea he was near as good as he is. He came on through training camp and just went on and on. He probably was the biggest surprise in our hockey club all year. He is a very mature hockey player. He is an amazing young hockey player and the greatest thing about him is that he shows great defensively. Most of the 18-year-old boys, all they think about is who gets the goal. They don't worry too much about their defensive game. They want to get attention. This kid, Marty, would rather go out and prevent a couple of goals than score a couple of goals.

"I've seen him when we win a hockey game six to two and he hasn't got a point and he's just overjoyed with the fact of winning. We lose a hockey game three to two and he's down in the dumps. When you get that kind of an attitude, you're a real winner!"

Gordie agreed that the comeback was a little tough on the old man, because of the legs and the wind. "When we travel on the day of a game, and we do a lot of that in this league, I'm not half what I should be. I never catch my wind. When the legs get tired I just go and sit down for awhile and come back out later. In the early days the legs never did get tired. Now it's the legs."

Howe noticed that the feeling of rivalry between teams was not as acrimonious in the W.H.A. as in the N.H.L. "One night in Vancouver I hit a guy and he got mad. He told me he had just lost an idol. Just because I hit him he doesn't like me. What I like is that most teams in our league are pretty closely matched. You never know which side is going to win."

John Wilson of the *Houston Chronicle* wrote in *Faceoff*

magazine: "... The Aeros completed a four-game sweep that made them champions of the W.H.A. in its second season of operation, a season marked by one of the most amazing individual comebacks in the annals of sport.

"It was the story of a 45-year-old man, playing a brutal young man's game at a level of competition no other man his age had ever dared to dream of. And he not only played the game magnificently, but he led his team to a championship.

"It was 'The Old Man' as they referred to him around the league who was the inspiration, the glue, the catalyst, the leader who brought the Aeros from a fourth-place finish in their maiden year to a league championship.

"The Old Man and his sons.

"Adding sheer preposterousness to the already incredible story of a middle-aged legend returning to the ice after a two years' absence was the fact that Howe joined his teenage sons in a storybook triumph.

"Mark 18 and Marty 19 lived up to their name.

"By the time the season opened, there was no question that the young Howes belonged, just as the scouting reports out of Canada had said. They didn't have to rely on the Howe name. The boys could skate and more than hold their own among men, rugged, experienced men.

"There was no falling back on the name for Gordie either. A lot of people thought there would be when he signed. Nobody can play big league hockey at 45—at least that was a widely-held opinion.

"But Gordie Howe could."

Mark Howe explained: "When people say, 'What are you doing out here? You're only trying to play because your Dad is Gordie Howe,' really that's the best thing people can do for me because I'm going to work twice as hard to prove to people around me that I can play. I owe a lot of being rookie of the year to my Dad because he can go in a corner and handle two guys and that leaves me out in front of the net and I'm left open."

Career Number Two

Marty: "I like checking and things, that's really the best part of the deal."

Mark has the forward and shooting skills of Gordie Howe, Marty has and likes the combat. He admits it. Someone asked Gordie Howe in Houston, "Are your elbows as sharp as ever?" Gordie could not hide the grin, as he replied, "I never used my elbows."

The Aeros' winning the Avco Cup "has to be the greatest thrill" for Gordie. "When you give up the game and then come back and play with your two sons and win the World Cup to boot, that has to be the greatest thrill.

"I came into this league with nothing to prove and I have nothing to prove next year. If I think I can help the team, I'll be back."

In their final year in Toronto, Marty and Mark had helped their Marlboros win the Memorial Cup, the championship. "The Memorial Cup was a thrill," agreed Mark, "but playing with the family and winning this was tops."

Hockey people use a plus and minus system to value-rate the players. All skaters on the ice when their team scores a goal get a plus. When a goal is scored by the other team they get a minus.

"Before the season started," Gordie said, "I gave myself a goal of 70 points and a plus score. I told Mark if he could score 25 goals and have a plus he would be helping the team and have a good season. I told Marty if he had a plus score it would be a successful season. I guess I set the goals too low."

Gordie finished with a plus 55, high on the team; Mark was second high with a plus 53 and Marty had a plus 38.

22

"Playing for My Country!"

Alongside the hockey rink in Saskatoon, Saskatchewan, Canada, Gordie Howe and his two sons would soon be taking to the ice in their Team Canada red, white, and blue uniforms with the maple leafs sewn on the sleeves along with the players' numerals.

"Three years ago when I was contemplating retirement I said I was giving up quite a bit, the fulfillment of a dream of playing with my two kids. At that time I didn't realize that with Team Canada [1972] I would have a shot at playing for my country against the Russians, and I had to give that up too. But, the fun of the game had left me, the fishing was wonderful, and that was what we were doing.

"At that particular time I was doing what I felt was best for myself and the fans.

"But all of a sudden I got rejuvenated because Houston picked up the two boys. I think I was doing a little bragging about that, so everything was just about perfect last year and I was going to retire this year, again.

"Then I got word that there would be a Team Canada and World Hockey Association would be associated with it, and also the owner of the Aeros would like me to participate for another year with the boys, to keep the fans coming so they can fill that new arena which is being built in Houston...."

That was why Gordie Howe decided to play a second year with the Aeros, so he and his two sons could represent his country playing against the Russians.

Anter the Houston Aeros had won the Avco Cup, the W.H.A. championship, the entire Howe family had been saluted at the Detroit and Windsor International Freedom Festival, receiving the Freedom Award, which had gone in previous years to people like President John F. Kennedy, Lowell Thomas, and Canada's Lester Pearson, as well as the American astronauts.

Now, he was about to play for his country, with his two native-born American sons, which created a bit of an international problem.

At first, the Russians balked because they remembered young Mark Howe on the United States Olympic Team at Sapporo back in the 1971-72 era. Eventually they agreed to recognize Marty and Mark Howe as Canadians because they were the sons of a native-born and still Canadian citizen.

Mark was asked, "What do you call No. 9 on the ice—Gordie or Dad?"

"Well, we don't have to yell at him much because he's got eyes all over his head. Most of the time I call him Gordie on the ice. He's definitely easy to work with. All you have to do is give him the puck and let him go."

Before joining Team Canada 74, Gordie underwent extensive physical tests at the Winnipeg Health Sciences Center and was proclaimed "a fantastic specimen" by Dr. Gerry Wilson. "We wanted to stress him maximally to see if he can function under a severe heart strain. He impressed us tremendously."

The Russian experience was different, but not altogether happy for Team Canada 74. "Some of the guys on Team Canada 72 told us we would have to restrain ourselves and it wouldn't be an easy thing to do," Gordie said.

The players were paid $5,000 each and the wives were invited to go along, something that had not been permitted in 1972.

Team Canada won some games, but the Russians won more. The hotel rooms in Russia had two kinds of bugs, the players said, the kind that crawl and the kind that eavesdrop.

The Team Canada players reported they would discover that the Russians' strategy completely changed the game after a Team Canada meeting in which their plans were discussed.

The Russians also learned. Sergei Kapustin followed Gordie Howe into the boards for a loose puck, and received an elbow massage instead, while Howe came out with the puck, passing to Bobby Hull for a goal.

About the bugs, Gordie said, "The only bugs I saw were the crawly type, but we never really took the trouble to search. We do know that one day we were complaining because there were no chairs and tables in the room, and the next day chairs and a table appeared, suddenly."

"No excuses, but the refereeing was atrocious. Still, the game is puck control and the Russians had it. We retaliated with maybe odd elbows or heavy body checks, but what the referees didn't see was quite a bit of kicking and an awful lot of hooking going on.

"I'm not going to cry about it. They had a tremendous team and we had to be at our best to beat them. And we weren't. I think the fever pitch explained it.

"When the national anthem was played in Quebec, you sang with so much pride and you just stood there and shivered in your boots. Then the puck felt like it was five pounds. I think the adrenaline had slowly leaked and we had to pump ourselves up again."

After the Russian series concluded, Team Canada went

to Czechoslovakia for an exhibition game. The Howes landed at Detroit's Metropolitan Airport on a Wednesday night, after going through seven time zones, and it was after midnight before they made their hotel for some rest.

The following night, they played with the Houston Aeros in an exhibition game against the new Michigan Stags and the Aeros won five to four, with two goals scored by Howe, along with one gloves-off scrap against Stags center J.P. LeBlanc, Howe landing about three blows to one as the crowd ate it up.

Jet lag hadn't slowed No. 9!

LeBlanc moaned, "You know Gordie. You go in a corner with him and he gives you a cheap shot. The referee standing right there and he gives me an elbow.

"I think those referees probably watched him when they were kids and he was a hero to them. It has to be really obvious before they call a penalty on him."

The same lament had been heard for years in the N.H.L., but as Bobby Hull once said, "I've enjoyed every high-sticking minute of it." They hate him and they love him.

Soon the 1974-75 World Hockey Association season would be officially underway.

Could Gordie Howe do it for another year? Could the Houston Aeros continue to be a championship team? Would this be the final year of regular competition for "the greatest of them all?"

Those were the questions, and the answers could only come in mid-1975, or later.

23

Another Milestone—
A Big One!

Near the end of the first season with the Houston Aeros in the W.H.A.—1973-74—Gordie Howe had passed the 800th goal milestone, finishing the season, his 26th year in pro hockey, with a career total of 1,737 games played, 817 goals scored, 1,092 assists, and 1,909 points scored, with 1,689 penalty minutes served.

Could a 46-, going on 47-, year-old man again come close to a 100-point season? Very doubtful. Gordie Howe needed 91 points, any combination of goals and assists that added up to 91, to hit the 2,000-point mark in professional major league hockey.

Bob Sicinski had been a center for the Chicago Cougars a year ago when the Aeros won the Avco Cup, four games to zip in the finals. Now he was with the brand new expansion Indianapolis Racers, about to meet the Aeros on the Indy home ice in October, 1974, the final exhibition game before the regular season.

"I don't know how much Gordie will play, because he just got back from Russia and they'll probably hold him out as much as possible to get ready for the season.

"But hockey isn't all on the ice. It wasn't only what he did on the ice last year that was so important for Houston, but what he did in the dressing room. He kept that team loose.

"With Gordie it goes deeper than just ability. He's an influence on the players, a leader. When he gets the puck, he controls it and he doesn't back off from anybody. He's got the respect of all other players and he uses it to his advantage.

"The Cougars got killed by Howe's power line. He isn't as fast as he used to be, but he can still turn it on and he still has his eyes.

"You've got to be able to come out of the corners with the puck and he does. He plays a good, tough game. He's just a super player. I would like to have seen him 10 years ago when he was in his real prime.

"Mark is going to be another Bobby Orr and Marty is super, too."

That from an opponent, an enemy who was defeated when the chips were down last spring. Bitter? Not so you could notice it.

Houston won two to one, Gordie assisting on a goal by Captain Ted Taylor.

The regular season started for the Aeros in Vancouver, where the three Howes contributed a goal and three assists to help the Aeros win the opener six to nothing. After playing with Team Canada in that country and in Russia, with side trips to other countries, then back home to the U.S. and Canada for five pre-season W.H.A. games and the first five regular season games on the road, the Howes finally returned to Howe-ston for a needed rest after 53 days on the road, by far the longest road trip ever for Gordie and probably any other player.

Another Milestone—A Big One!

In November, back in Indianapolis, Mark Howe scored his first three-goal hat trick against the Aeros, while brother Marty got one, his third of the year, with Gordie contributing a pair of assists. The Aeros beat the Racers ten to nothing.

In December, Mark and Gordie led an attack against their old goalie teammate Smokey McLeod, since traded to the Vancouver Blazers, beating the Blazers five to two, after Vancouver had Houston down two to one. Mark scored the tying goal and Gordie put the team ahead minutes later.

They hadn't forgotten Gordie back in Detroit, either, as a young fellow named Scott Bondy was selected to receive the 1974 Gordie Howe Scholarship, which Bruce Norris of the Red Wings continued to maintain. Bondy was a freshman at the University of Michigan and played left wing on the Wolverines collegiate hockey team.

In the meantime, Gordie announced that he would play one game in the 1975-76 season, the opening night of the brand new 18,000-seat Houston Aeros stadium, the "Summit."

"It would be a shame to call yourself a Houston Aero without the opportunity to play at least one game there. If I can read a blueprint, this building is going to be second to none."

Actually, what Gordie was saying—what his announcement really means—is that he would have to go through all the rigors of training camp, make the pre-season regimen, to play that one game. No way could he just put on the leathers and the pads for one game. He would have to go through the worst of a new season just to be ready.

The Aeros were on another winning streak, more on the road than at home. "We're playing better hockey on the road," Gordie explained, "because we just seem to get more involved. It seems like we're gambling a little more at home and getting burned because of it."

Shortly after the Howes had torn the final page off the

1974 calendar and hung up the fresh one, Gordie admitted that old man Time was beginning to take his toll, as he must with all men, especially those who play a young man's sporting game—game? Hell, this is war.

"The pains seem to get worse after every game. I find it really tough to get up the next morning after a game and it's really bad when we play two or three games in a row."

When Coach Bill Dineen calls for a practice the morning after a night game, Gordie is there 99 percent of the time. No favors asked, as Dineen pointed out, "Gordie always felt he had to set the example and he still does."

By mid-season Dineen had cut down Gordie's game time on the ice, from the usual 30 to 40 minutes, to about 18 minutes in a game. When the power play was called for, Gordie often appeared as the penalty killer.

"There's no question that Gordie has slowed up," commented a former teammate, Johnny Wilson, a rival coach with the Michigan Stags and later the Baltimore team in the W.H.A. "But he still glides all over the ice and when he has to be some place to make the big play, he's there."

By the All-Star break, the Houston Aeros were out in front, looking like another championship team. About his former teammate and now coach, Dineen, Howe said, "The thing I like about Foxey is that when he gets mad he doesn't say anything. The madder he gets the quieter he gets.

"The pressure in the N.H.L. was such that if you're behind one goal, you come into the dressing room and the coach may be throwing oranges at you. Foxey may throw oranges, but he makes them nice, soft pitches so you can eat them later."

John Schella, an Aeros defenseman, suggested the credit for the Aeros success this way: "One of the big reasons why we are doing so well is that we've got such a close-knit team. We're together off the ice and when we get on the ice we get it on."

Frank Hughes added, "We are a team, team. We aren't worried about individual records."

Another Milestone—A Big One!

In Edmonton Coliseum, Alberta, Canada, Gordie Howe said "it was fun" playing in his final All-Star game in pro hockey, after his goal and an assist helped his West team beat the East six to four, before a capacity 15,326 fans.

"Sure it's nice to wind up with one for the road, but the real highlight was to have the kid score one," after Mark had taken a pass from Gordie for the first marker of the game.

The senior Howe's score came late in the game, a weak backhand pass that happened to roll behind the East goaltender Andy Brown, a former Red Wing now with the Indy Racers.

"What a shot!" Gordie exclaimed in a kidding boast about the admittedly weak shot. "Did anyone notice if it made it to the back of the net?"

Gordie was turning on the play and did not know he had scored until Andy Brown shouted, "You lucky old [deleted]!" Howe had broken in on the Red Wings team with Adam Brown, Andy's father, then watched Andy in his rookie year with the Wings in 1971-72, Gordie's first year of retirement number one.

"It's hard to say how much Gordie means to hockey," said André Lacroix, an All-Star teammate. "He's the star of every game. He's still at it at 46 and he's the greatest that ever lived."

Early in March, 1975, World Hockcy Association President Dennis Murphy announced the league's Most Valuable Player cup, which Gordie had won last year, will henceforth be known as the Gordie Howe Cup, a signal honor.

A couple of weeks later, Gordie scored his 30th goal of the season, playing against the Toronto Toros. The Aeros lost the game, five to four, but the Toros proudly proclaimed the new regular season attendance record of 15,517 paid customers. The all-time W.H.A. attendance mark is 17,211, April 28, 1974, in a playoff game at St. Paul's Civic Center, the game between the Minnesota Fighting Saints and who? . . . the Houston Aeros, who else? The Howes draw in the customers.

March 19, 1975, at Sam Houston Coliseum, Mark Howe scored his 27th and 28th goals of the season, against the Indy Racers.

Nine nights later, Thursday, March 27, 1975, Gordie Howe reached and topped that huge, towering milestone, the 2,000th point in major league hockey, and he did it at home against the Winnipeg Jets and Bobby Hull, the Aeros winning eight to zip.

Gordie's 31st goal of the season came little more than 11 seconds into the first period. The Aeros were playing short-handed at the time and Howe skated around Bobby Hull to fire the puck into the net, giving him 1,997 points for the career to that moment.

The second goal came nine seconds into the third period, giving the Aeros a five to nothing lead, and Gordie 1,999 points.

Just 27 seconds later, Howe centered to Jim Sherrit, who scored, giving Howe his 2,000th point for the assist. Gordie swooped into the net and grabbed the souvenir puck as the fans gave him a standing ovation.

Gordie's sixth point of the night came when he presented an assist to Mark's 32nd goal of the season, Gordie now officially at 2,001 points. That game clinched the Western Division championship for the Aeros as well.

Old nemesis Bobby Hull was, at that point, runner-up to Howe in career points at 1,428, a good five or six years away from 2,000.

After smashing the 2,000 barrier, Gordie said, "It was good to get it on a night when everything fell into place. I felt good when we were skating in warmup and my legs felt good. I told Mark it was going to be a 'skate night.' It all adds up to the enjoyment of the game. The 2,000th came on a good night. We clinched the title in our league. I don't think anybody can catch us as far as the overall best record. Larry Lund gets 100 points for the first time in his life and

Another Milestone—A Big One! 195

young Sherrit gets his 20th goal. You can't ask for much more."

Actually, Sherrit, aware that this was his 20th goal, a personal triumph, was ready to claim the puck for his own trophy room, but the young fellow didn't have a chance. "I've never seen Gordie move so fast," Sherrit said. "He was in and out of that net like a shot. It surprised me, but I soon realized what was going on."

Gordie continued: "But the thing that hits you is a chance to play again. I've said before that these have been the two most enjoyable years of my career, because I gave it all up and then came back."

He remembers his first goal. "It was against Turk Broda in 1946 at Detroit. It was a rebound. I happened to be on the left side and shot into an almost open net. It came in the second period and the game ended in a three-three tie with Toronto. I wrote 15 letters home that night, that's why I remember it.

"I never thought about anything like this [his 2,001 points]. I never dreamed of lasting longer than one year with the Aeros, but this was like a lollipop waiting to be plucked. I had to grab for it.

"I have to remember the bad nights, too. I guess mere longevity will get you records," continued the still modest Howe.

The game left old nemesis Bobby Hull scoreless with a season record of 72 goals in 72 games, looking for at least 77 to set a new record, possibly 78 in the 78 games.

When the season ended, Hull had broken the 76-goal record set by Phil Esposito of the Boston Bruins in the N.H.L. Hull scored his 77th goal in the final game, a five-to-five tie against San Diego. The *Hockey News* voted Hull the Player of the Year in the W.H.A., although his Winnipeg Jets failed to make the playoffs.

In the Aeros' final game of the year, they bowed to the

Baltimore Blades four to two, as Gordie Howe scored his 34th goal of the season, midway in the final period. Quite possibly his final regular season goal ever.

This is the 1974-75 W.H.A. record for Bobby Hull and the Howes:

	Games	Goals	Assists	Points	Penalty Minutes
Bobby Hull	78	77	65	142	41
Gordie Howe	75	34	65	99	84
Mark Howe	74	36	40	76	30
Marty Howe	75	13	21	34	89

Gordie Howe scored 2,008 points in his 27-season career. Bobby Hull has scored 1,493 points in 18 seasons.

Here are the career totals, to date:

	Games	Goals	Assists	Points	Penalty Minutes
Gordie Howe	1,832	851	1,157	2,008	1,773
Bobby Hull	1,652	785	708	1,493	756

The Aeros headed into the playoffs, hoping for a repeat victory in the Avco Cup finals.

In the playoffs, the Houston Aeros beat Cleveland four games to one; then they skated all over San Diego four games straight and in the finals, the Aeros won four straight over Quebec to capture their second consecutive Avco Cup World Hockey Association championship.

Meanwhile, Gordie Howe was losing two old Detroit Red Wings team records, for the most assists and the most points in a season, established in 1968-69, 59 assists and 103 points.

It was 24-year-old Marcel Dionne, who had been fired for 10 minutes late in 1974, but who was then reinstated when he apologized for telling a reporter the Wings were a team of losers.

Another Milestone—A Big One!

Since the firing and reinstatement, Dionne bounced back and turned in the best year ever for a Red Wing, with 44 goals, 74 assists and 118 points, third high in the N.H.L.

Gordie's Red Wings mark of 49 goals was shattered by young Danny Grant who scored 50, crediting the help of Dionne's assists.

The recent years have been big scoring seasons in both the N.H.L. and the W.H.A. with 49-goal and 102-point seasons long gone, but it will be almost five years, at least, before anyone reaches that 2,000 plateau.

Even then, there will be thousands who will remember and insist that others "can have their choice of all the rest, 'Cause if you're a Howe fan, you've got the very best!"